CW00482487

1

CONTENTS

Introduction

Background

Highlights

Exploring the city

Museums

Monuments and sights of interest

Excursions

Directory

Index

The capital of Andalucía is a city of art and history which has managed to maintain its magnificent traditions without turning its back on modernity. Sevilla has been described as a feminine city which is fully aware of its charms and is happy to display them to its visitors. The *sevillanos* are passionate about where they live and take every opportunity to extol its many virtues. However, Sevilla is more than just a city: it is a way of embracing life to the full in the exuberant, festive and, above all, passionate manner for which it is famous.

Sevilla is many things, perhaps too many to highlight in just a few words: it is the Guadalquivir, a river that has left its indelible mark on the city's history and acts as a mirror in which to look into its past and future; it is its impressive Holy Week and April Fair; it is Velázquez, Murillo, Don Juan Tenorio and Carmen; the scent of orange blossom; the lively gatherings of friends; and the dancing of *sevillanas* and bullfights. Sevilla is bright, it is colourful, and, in summer, it is extremely hot!

J. Bouraly/MICHELIN

Introduction

Cathedral

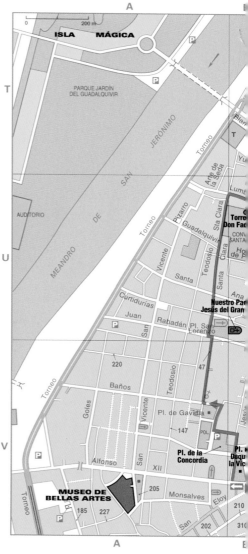

6

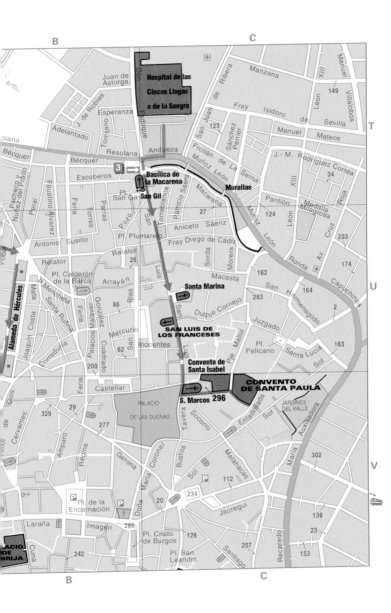

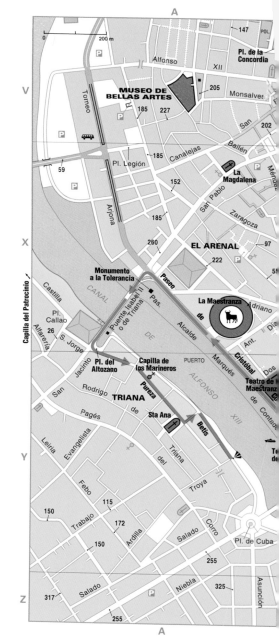

See "Exploring the City"

1 El Palacio de San Telmo y el Parque de María Luisa

2 Paseo junto al río

3 La Macarena y la calle San Luis

4 Centro

5 De la plaza del duque de la Victoria a la Alameda de Hércules

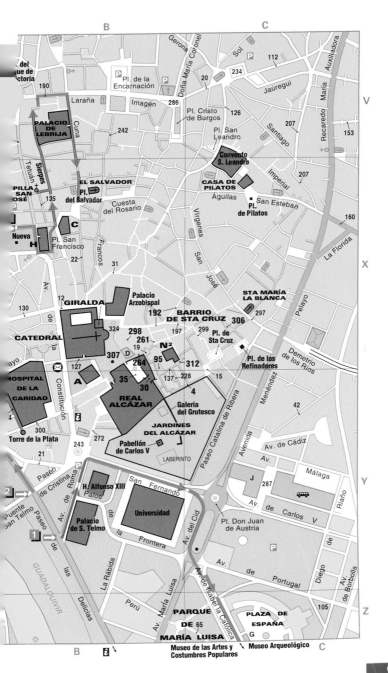

Parque del Duque de Victoria — 190

B — Gerona — Maria Coronel — Sol — 112 — C

Pl. de la Encarnación

Doña Maria Coronel — 20 — 234 — Jáuregui

Recaredo — Maria — Auxiliadora

V

Laraña — Imagen — 286

PALACIO DE LEBRIJA

Cuna — 242

Pl. Cristo de Burgos — 126 — Pl. San Leandro — Santiago — 207 — 153

Sierpes — Tetuán

PILLA SAN JOSÉ — 135

EL SALVADOR — Pl. del Salvador

Cuesta del Rosario

Convento S. Leandro

Imperial — 207

Nueva — C — H — Pl. San Francisco — 22

Francos — 31

CASA DE PILATOS

Águilas — San Esteban — Pl. de Pilatos

160 — La Florida

X

Virgenes

San José

12 — GIRALDA — Palacio Arzobispal — 192

130 — de — la

324 — 298 — 261 — 19 — 197 — 299 — Pl. de Sta Cruz

STA MARÍA LA BLANCA — 306 — 297

BARRIO DE STA CRUZ

Pelayo

Demétrio de los Ríos

CATEDRAL

307 — D — N² — 95 — 264 — 312

127 — A — 137 — 228 — 15

Pl. de los Refinadores

HOSPITAL DE LA CARIDAD — 35 — 30

REAL ALCÁZAR

4 — Galería del Grutesco

Menéndez — 42

Constitución

Pelayo — 4 — 300

Torre de la Plata — 21

JARDINES DEL ALCÁZAR

Paseo Catalina de Ribera

272 — 243

Pabellón de Carlos V

LABERINTO

Av. de Cádiz

Av.

Avenida

Paseo de Cristina

H. Alfonso XIII — San Fernando

Palos

J — 287 — Málaga

Riaño

Y

Puente San Telmo — Paseo

Av. de Roma

Palacio de S. Telmo

Universidad

Frontera

Av. del Cid

Av. de Carlos V

Pl. Don Juan de Austria

de

Diego

GUADALQUIVIR

Delicias

La Rábida

Perú

Frontera

Av. de María Luisa

Av.

de

Portugal

Av. de Botbolla

Av. de Isabela Católica

105

Z

PARQUE DE 65 MARÍA LUISA

PLAZA DE ESPAÑA

G

B — Museo de las Artes y Costumbres Populares — Museo Arqueológico — C

9

G. Bludzin/MICHELIN

Detail, Casa de Pilatos

11

M ichelin Sevilla city plan 74. Population: 701 927. Michelin map 578 T 11–12. Located at the heart of the Guadalquivir plain, Sevilla is the hub of an excellent network of motorways and main roads linking it with other Andalusian towns and cities, including Huelva (92km/57mi W), Jerez de la Frontera (90km/56mi S), Cádiz (123km/77mi SW), Córdoba (143km/89mi NE), Málaga (211km/132mi SE) and Granada (250km/ 156mi E).

🗏 *Avenida de la Constitución, 21, ☎ 954 22 14 04; Plaza Triunfo, 1-3, 41004, ☎ 954 21 00 05; Paseo de las Delicias, 9, ☎ 954 23 44 65.*

Imagen © TURISMO ANDALUZ S.A.

Location

El Guadalquivir and the Torre del oro

Background

Historical outline

"*Hércules me construyó, Julio César me rodeó de murallas y altas torres y el Rey Santo me conquistó*" (Hercules built me; Caesar surrounded me with walls and towers; and the King Saint conquered me), says the inscription on the former Jerez Gate (Puerta de Jerez), destroyed in the 19C. From the earliest times the history of Sevilla has been determined by its existence as a river port. Although its origins are less than clear, it is thought that the city was founded by Iberians. It later became a Greek, Phoenician and Carthaginian colony, which was subsequently overrun by the Romans in 205 BC following a long siege.

H. Belmenouar/MICHELIN

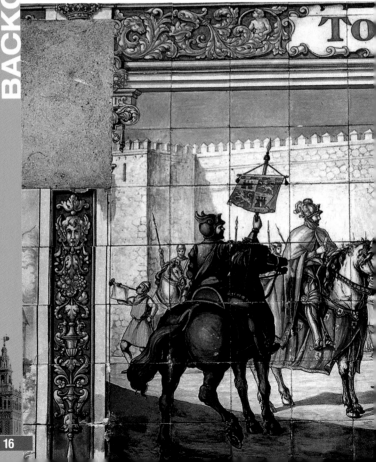

Romans and Visigoths

The first stage of Roman occupation was marked by internal disputes between various factions. However, in 42 BC, the city was conquered by Julius Caesar, who built its fortifications and presided over a period of great splendour, transforming it into one of the main cities in Baetica.

In the 5C the Vandals invaded the region; they were subsequently expelled by the Visigoths who made the city the capital of their kingdom until the court was transferred to Toledo. The 6C saw the rise of a figure of major importance, the bishop St Isidore, author of *Etymologies*, who was to have great influence on medieval European culture.

The Moors

The conquest by the Moors in 712 heralded the start of a long period of Arab domination. During the Caliphate, the city came under the control of Córdoba; upon its fall in 1031 it became a taifa king-

Azulejos, Plaza de España

NO MADEJA DO = NO ME HA DEJADO

This emblem on the city's coat of arms was given to Sevilla by Alfonso X the Wise (1221-84) to commemorate the loyalty and support he had received from the city. The figure of eight in the emblem, representing a skein of wool *(madeja)*, creates the motto "No madeja do" or "No me ha dejado", which translates as "It has not forsaken me".

dom. During the reign of Al Mutamid, Sevilla experienced a period of great cultural development. However, the difficult relations with the Christian king, Alfonso VI, resulted in his asking for help from the Almoravids who subsequently seized control of the kingdom in 1091. In the 12C, the Almohads seized control from the Almoravids and instigated a period of urban development, including the construction of both the Giralda and the *mezquita* (mosque), on the site now occupied by the cathedral.

Imagen © TURISMO ANDALUZ S.A.

The Reconquest

On 23 November 1248, Fernando III the Saint reconquered Sevilla and established his court in the city. Alfonso X the Wise and Pedro I did likewise, with the latter restoring and subsequently residing in the Alcázar.

The Golden Age

Following the discovery of America in 1492, Sevilla developed a monopoly on trade with the New World and became the departure and arrival point for every expedition to the newly discovered conti-

nent. Many expeditions departed from the city, including those by Amerigo Vespucci, and Magellan, who set out in 1519 and whose expedition was the first to circumnavigate the globe. 1503 saw the founding of the **Casa de Contratación**, a body established to encourage, inspect and control trade with the Americas.

Sevilla began to amass great wealth, as foreign merchants and bankers became increasingly attracted by thoughts of American gold. Palaces were built, new industries were created and the smell of money and frenetic activity attracted hustlers, villains and people from every sector of society. The population of Sevilla almost doubled during the course of the 16C, rising to a figure of some 200 000 inhabitants.

The decline

Following the plague of 1649, the city entered a period of decline which was exacerbated by the transfer of the Casa de Contratación to Cádiz in 1717.

20C

During the course of the 20C Sevilla hosted two major international exhibitions: the 1929 Ibero-American Exhibition and Expo'92, both of which were to have a significant effect on the layout of the city.

Expo'92 saw the realisation of a number of large projects, in particular the Isla de la Cartuja, the site on which the fair was held. The Isla Mágica theme park and the Centro Andaluz de Arte Contemporáneo are now housed on the site.

La Cartuja

17c Sevillan painting

The 17C is without doubt the Golden Age of Andalusian painting, which started out loyal to the dominant Flemish tradition of the 16C before developing its own expression through opulence and light. From the middle of the century onwards, Sevilla and Madrid became the undisputed capitals of Spanish painting.

The renown of Sevillian artists in the early decades of the 17C, such as **Francisco Pacheco**, the father-in-law of Velázquez, has remained obscured by the brilliance of three undisputed masters: Velázquez, Zurbarán and Murillo.

Diego Velázquez spent the majority of his professional life in Madrid as a portrait painter to the Court. However, neither fame nor the influence of Italian artists whom he admired greatly, in particular Titian, could bring him to forget his training in Sevilla. It was during this period (1617-23), before he left the city of his birth, that he painted works with predominantly religious themes and or in the costumbrismo genre (Adoration of the Kings, Museo del Prado, Madrid).

Francisco de Zurbarán (1598-1664), from Extremadura, interpreted themes of monastic life, but also painted more popular themes, representing reality as accurately as possible, with an economy of means and a deliberately limited range of colour which emphasises the play of light and, in his portraits in particular, sees his characters burst forth from the canvas. His academy rapidly developed into one of the largest in Sevilla, exporting more works to the Americas than any other in the city.

Bartolomé Esteban Murillo (1617-82), whose works of a religious nature (Virgin Mary, Infant Jesus) have been reproduced time and time again, was the most famous Spanish artist of the period. Through his academy, he also exported innumerable canvases destined for the churches of the New World. The delicate touch and warmth of these occasionally bland paintings cannot hide the qualities of an extraordinary painter who was a great master of both technique and colour, and highly skilled in the portrayal of genre scenes.

In complete contrast, **Juan Valdés Leal** (1662-95) concentrated on expression and the macabre with a striking power and realism that at times touched on the morbid, as seen in the frescoes painted for the city's Hospital de la Caridad.

Virgin by Zurbarán

Fiestas

During the spring, Sevilla lives for the two fiestas that have brought it international fame: Holy Week *(Semana Santa)* and the April Fair *(Feria de Abril)*. For those who have yet to experience either, it is difficult to imagine their splendour or the way in which the city's inhabitants embrace them. These two events are the two sides of the same coin: two authentic, yet totally distinct forms of expression of the Sevillian soul.

Semana Santa

Holy Week is celebrated between Palm Sunday and Easter Sunday, either in March or April, depending on the liturgical calendar. The origins of Sevilla's Semana Santa date back to the 16C, a time when the first brotherhoods or fraternities were formed to provide assistance for guild associations. Over 50 brotherhoods participate in the Holy Week processions, each carrying its own statue of Christ or the Virgin Mary.

The whole city comes out onto the street during this ceremony to relive the Passion of Christ and the pain of his mother. The spectacle is an impressive one, with the streets and street corners of the city providing a magnificent backdrop to these processions. During this extravagant religious ritual, with its breathtakingly beautiful statues atop floats exquisitely adorned with gold and silver, popular fervour comes to the fore in an atmosphere bordering on ecstasy.

The processions – These take place throughout the course of the week. Every brotherhood leaves its own church or chapel and usually carries two floats or *pasos*: one bearing Christ, the other the Virgin Mary. They make one journey *(carrera)* to the cathedral and then return to their headquarters. Each float passes along the calle Sierpes and in front of the town hall. The hundred or more floats winding their way through the city's streets, accompanied by a band of musicians, are carried by *costaleros* – young men under the tutelage of an overseer *(capataz)* – who take immense pride in transporting these holy figures and demonstrate great skill and physical prowess in this feat of endurance.

A number of these famous processions take place on the **madrugá** (the early morning of Good Friday): El Silencio, La Macarena, La Esperanza de Triana, Los Gitanos and, on the Friday afternoon, El Cachorro. Some of the statues borne aloft in procession are priceless works of art by leading 17C sculptors, including *Jesus of Great Power* and *Christ of Love*, by Juan de Mesa; the *Christ of the Passion*, by Martínez Montañés; *La Macarena*, by an unknown artist; the *Holy Christ of the Expiration* ("El Cachorro"), by Francisco Antonio Gijón; and *Our Father Jesus of Nazareth*, by Francisco Ocampo.

Feria de Abril

Founded in the middle of the 19C as an animal fair, the April Fair soon set aside its

role as a market, developing into a colourful and lively fair with its emphasis on pure enjoyment. The Feria is the major fiesta held in Sevilla, a city with a reputation for partying like nowhere else on Earth.

The April Fair takes place two or three weeks after Holy Week in the Los Remedios district, where a veritable city of light is created, illuminated by thousands of bulbs and fairy lights, with a network of streets housing the traditional *casetas*. The festivities commence late on Monday evening and in the early hours of Tuesday morning with the illumination of the fairground area, and continue until the following Sunday when a firework display draws events to a close.

During the *feria* the streets of the fairground are thronged with a high-spirited and good-humoured crowd, while inside the *casetas* the famous *fino* sherry from Jerez and *manzanilla* from Sanlúcar flow abundantly, tapas are eaten, and *sevillanas* are danced with great passion until the early hours.

During the day, the women of

Night-time during la Feria

Sevilla do their best to upstage each other with the beauty and grace of their flamenco costumes as they dance, stroll through the streets of the city with their friends and family, or wander around the *feria* area itself. The parade is another attractive feature of this unique fiesta, with Andalusian horsemen dressed in their typical, tight-fitting costumes and wide-brimmed *sombreros cordobeses*, and carriages pulled by horses with their colourful harnesses.

The calle del Infierno in the *feria* precinct is also a popular aspect of this annual event with its range of attractions for young and old alike.

El Rocío

The list of local fiestas would not be complete without mention of **El Rocío**. This religious pilgrimage, a combination of Marian devotion and festive spirit, converges on a chapel in the village of El Rocío, to the south of Almonte in the province of Huelva.

With its numerous brotherhoods, Sevilla is actively involved in this *romería*, in which pilgrims travel on foot, horseback or by cart, following the float or *simpecado*, which bears the standard of the Virgin. During the journey, these pilgrims sing and dance special pilgrimage *sevillanas* in honour of the Virgin Mary.

Flamenco

Flamenco was created towards the middle of the 19C from a combination of pre-existing musical forms with Jewish, Byzantine, Moorish and even Hindu influence. Experts fail to agree on the scale of this influence, but what does seem clear is that it developed in Lower Andalucía (Jerez, Utrera, Lebrija, Cádiz etc) via a number of families who passed on the art from generation to generation. Although it has been admitted that flamenco is not gypsy in origin, the gitanos have incorporated their own personality and their considerable interpretative capacity into flamenco.

For a long time considered to be an art form associated with those of "ill repute" – a view expressed at the turn of the century by writers such as Miguel de Unamuno – initiatives led by leading cultural figures such as Federico García Lorca and Manuel de Falla elevated flamenco to the status of the cultural expression of the Andalusian people.

Since that time, flamenco has seen the rise to fame of singers such as Antonio Mairena, Fosforito, la Niña de la Puebla and, in more recent times, Camarón de la Isla, renowned guitarists such as Paco de Lucía and dancers of the quality of Cristina Hoyos.

The new generations have demonstrated that flamenco remains a living art and that it is capable of evolving and assimilating new rhythms. Purists do not agree, but groups such as Ketama and Navajita Pleteá, guitarists such as Raimundo Amador and dancers of international renown such as Joaquín Cortés and Antonio Canales are ready to show that flamenco is able to explore new avenues.

Although to many observers and listeners the individual aspects of flamenco may be somewhat difficult to comprehend and interpret, it is impossible not to be moved by the passion of this truly Andalusian art form.

FLAMENCO COSTUME

What is considered to be the Andalusian costume *par excellence* is the one traditionally worn in Córdoba and Sevilla, which saw various modifications during the second half of the 20C. In fact, the so-called Andalusian costume is perhaps the only one in the world with its own fashion, which varies from year to year in terms of its colour, number and length of pleated ruffles, the shape of the sleeves etc.

Variations apart, the **traje de faralaes** or flamenco costume worn by women is characterised by bright colours and a tight-fitting design which highlights the figure; and the wide neck and ruffles which finish off the inner part of the dress add to the attractive look. The costume is sometimes accompanied by a shawl, earrings and bracelets of similar colour to the dress, as well as real or artificial flowers in the hair. When on horseback, the campero costume is worn, consisting of an equestrian skirt, a blouse with a lace apron, and a black jacket.

The men's costume, generally black, grey or dark brown in colour, consists of a short jacket, white shirt without a tie, tight-fitting trousers and leather boots. The traditional headgear is either the wide-brimmed *sombrero cordobés* or the lower-crowned *sombrero sevillano*.

Mattes/MICHELIN

Highlights

The Giralda and cathedral★★★

Giralda★★★

The impressive and elegant Giralda is the symbol of the city. Built at the end of the 12C, this brick minaret (96m/315ft), part of the old mosque (mezquita), was surmounted by three gilded spheres which sadly fell off as a result of the earthquake which struck Sevilla in the 14C. It acquired its present appearance in the 16C when the Cordoban architect Hernán Ruiz added the belfry, the three superimposed stages and the balconies. These were then crowned with an enormous weather vane, the statue of Faith, popularly known as the Giraldillo (from girar: to turn), from which the name of the tower has evolved.

The tower is a masterpiece of Almohad art, with the delicate yet restrained decoration so typical of this purist, austere dynasty, which shunned ostentation, yet still managed to create a harmonious style combining beauty and simplicity. The decoration on each of the four sides is organised into three vertical registers with panels of sebka decoration. Access to the Giralda is from inside the cathedral (see below).

Cathedral★★★

☎ 954 21 49 71.

Visit – "Let us build a cathedral so immense that we will be taken for madmen", the chapter is said to have declared in 1401 when it ordered the demolition of the mosque and the construction of the new cathedral. The cathedral is impressive in its dimensions, and in terms of floor space it is considered to be the third largest in the Christian world after St Peter's in the Vatican and St Paul's in London. As one of the last Gothic cathedrals to be built in Spain it shows obvious Renaissance influence.

Viewing the massive **exterior** makes it possible to appreciate the full extent of its size. The Cristóbal (or Príncipe), Asunción and Concepción (in the Patio de los Naranjos) doorways are modern (19C and 20C), yet respect the style of the cathedral as a whole, while the Puerta del Nacimiento and Puerta del Bautismo, which open out onto the Avenida de la Constitución, include beautiful sculptures by Mercadante de Bretaña (1460). At the east end of the cathedral admire the rounded Chapel Royal (Capilla Real – 1575), decorated with coats of arms and, on either side, the Gothic Puerta de Palos and Puerta de las Campanillas with Renaissance-style tympana in which Miguel Perrin has made full play of perspective.

Entrance through puerta San Cristóbal.

Interior – This universe of stone, stained glass and grilles is striking in its size and richness, while its extraordinary height is the result of its tall, slender pillars. The ground plan consists of five aisles

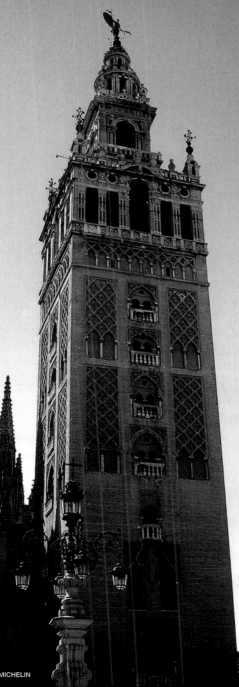

Cathedral exterior

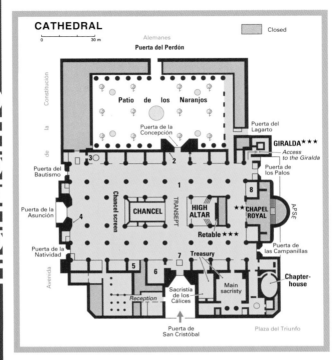

CATHEDRAL

0 ———— 30 m

Closed

Alemanes

Puerta del Perdón

Constitución

la

de

Puerta del Bautismo

Puerta de la Asunción

Puerta de la Natividad

Avenida

Patio de los Naranjos

Puerta de la Concepción

3

2

1

Chancel screen

CHANCEL

TRANSEPT

HIGH ALTAR

Retable ★★★

Puerta del Lagarto

GIRALDA ★★★

Access to the Giralda

Puerta de los Palos

8

★★ **CHAPEL ROYAL**

APSE

Puerta de las Campanillas

4

5   6

7   **Treasury**

Reception

Sacristía de los Cálices

Main sacristy

Chapter-house

Puerta de San Cristóbal

Plaza del Triunfo

– the central nave being wider and of greater height – with chapels in the side aisles. The column shafts support simple Flamboyant Gothic pointed vaults, except in the central section. The vault of the transept, also Flamboyant in style, reaches a height of 56m/184ft. A **mirror** *(1)* on the floor provides visitors with a striking view of these magnificent stone vaults.

Climbing the Giralda – It is possible to climb up to the tower's belfry (70m/230ft)

via a ramp with **34** sections. The ascent is slow, although not particularly difficult; take your time to admire the views of the Patio de los Naranjos, the gargoyles and pinnacles of the cathedral and the Alcázar from the balconies on the way up. Your efforts will be well rewarded once you reach the outer platform at the top with a magnificent **panorama★★★** over the city.

Chancel – The chancel *(capilla mayor)*, unbelievably rich

THE "SEISES" – A FINE TRADITION

The Seises are a group of 12 brightly dressed choir boys who perpetuate a tradition dating back to the 16C, by which they sing and dance in front of the cathedral's high altar during the eight days following Corpus Christi and the Feast of the Immaculate Conception. Initially the group consisted of 6 *(seis)* boys, hence the name. They also accompany the **Corpus Christi** procession when this stops in the plaza del Ayuntamiento and the plaza del Salvador.

in decoration, is enclosed by a splendid 16C **Plateresque grille****, by Fray Francisco de Salamanca. The immense Flemish **altarpiece***** (1482-1525), the largest in Spain, is profusely and delicately carved with a number of colourful scenes from the lives of Christ and the Virgin Mary, with the exception of the predella which is decorated with saints. The altarpiece has seven vertical panels, the widest of which is in the centre. Unfortunately, it is impossible to get close enough to admire what is one of the world's most impressive altarpieces.

Choir – In the central nave, partly hidden by a 16C grille by Fray Francisco de Salamanca is the *coro*, with its fine 15C and 16C stalls. The majestic organs date from the 18C. The **trascoro**, a chancel screen of multicoloured marble, jasper and bronze, is 17C.

Treasury – The treasury is in the 16C **Sacristía de los Cálices** (Chalice Sacristy), and is surmounted by a fine vault. A number of interesting paintings are exhibited here: *Santa Justa and Santa Rufina* by Goya, a Zurbarán, a triptych by Alejo Fernández and several canvases by Valdés Leal. The anteroom of the sacristy houses the **Tenebrario**, a 7.80m/25ft, fifteen-branch Plateresque candelabrum, used during Holy Week processions.

The **main sacristy** (*sacristía mayor*), a fine 16C room with the floor plan of a Greek cross, contains the impressive Renaissance silver **monstrance** (*custodia*) by Juan de Arfe, measuring 3.90m/13ft and weighing 475kg/1 045lb; a *Santa Teresa* by Zurbarán and *The Martyrdom of San Lorenzo* by Lucas Jordán can be seen on the rear wall.

Chapter house – The chapter house (*sala capitular*), a fine example of 16C Renaissance architecture, has an elliptical dome and a characteristic *Immaculate Conception* by Murillo.

Capilla Real** – *Closed to visitors*. The Chapel Royal was built during the reign of Charles V over an earlier

CHAPELS AND ALTARS
Once you have seen the cathedral's major works, make sure you spend some time admiring some of its chapels, which themselves contain numerous works of art.

– **Altar de Nuestra Señora de Belén (2)** (Our Lady of Bethlehem): on the north side, to the left of the Puerta de la Concepción. A fine portrayal of the Virgin Mary by Alonso Cano.

– **Capilla de San Antonio (3)**: this chapel contains several interesting canvases dominated by Murillo's *Vision of St Anthony of Padua*, on the right-hand wall. Also worthy of note are *The Baptism of Christ*, also by Murillo, and two paintings of St Peter by Valdés Leal.

– **Altar del Santo Ángel (4)** (at the foot of the cathedral, to the left of the Puerta Mayor): this altar is dominated by a fine *Guardian Angel* by Murillo.

– **Capilla de San Hermenegildo (5)** (next to the Capilla de San José): the 15C alabaster tomb of Cardinal Cervantes sculpted by Lorenzo Mercadante.

– **Capilla de la Virgen de la Antigua (6)** (the next chapel): larger than the others and covered with an elevated vault. A fine 14C fresco of the Virgin adorns the altar.

– **19C funerary monument to Christopher Columbus (7)**: the explorer's coffin is borne by four pallbearers bearing the symbols of Castilla, León, Navarra and Aragón on their chest.

– **Capilla de San Pedro (8)**: the walls of this chapel are hung with a superb series of paintings by **Zurbarán** illustrating the life of St Peter.

chapel. The monumental size of this Plateresque chapel, accessed via a huge arch, is particularly impressive. Square in shape, it is covered by an elegant, richly ornamented coffered dome with carved busts and contains a small apse which is itself covered by a scallop shell decorated with figures. A wooden carving of the **Virgen de los Reyes**, the patron saint of Sevilla, decorates the altar, behind which, in a silver urn of great value, are the remains of Fernando III the Saint. On either side are the tombs of Alfonso X and that of his mother, Beatrice of Swabia. The Capilla Real is enclosed by a majestic grille dating from 1771.

Patio de los Naranjos – This exceptional rectangular patio, on the north side of the cathedral, is planted with orange trees (naranjos) and was the patio used for ritual ablutions in the former mosque.

Exit the Patio de los Naranjos through the Puerta del Perdón.

Puerta del Perdón – The Almohad arch and the door leaves are original features of this majestic entrance to the patio of the former mosque. The impressive sculptures and the relief, representing the Expulsion of the Money Changers from the Temple, were created in the 16C.

Palacio Arzobispal

The residence of the Archbishop of Sevilla is situated in the attractive plaza de la Virgen de los Reyes, with its monumental lantern and numerous horse-drawn carriages awaiting customers. The edifice has an elegant, late-Baroque façade built at the beginning of the 18C.

Plaza de Santa Marta

Take the narrow callejón de Santa Marta, opposite the Palacio Arzobispal. The alleyway offers the only access to this delightful small square, with its whitewashed façades, simple wrought-iron grilles and a small stone cross shaded by orange trees. The charming, hushed atmosphere found here is typical of that found in so many of the city's squares.

Archivo General de Indias

The historical archives relating to the Spanish conquest of the Americas are housed in the former Exchange (lonja), built at the end of the 16C according to plans by Juan de Herrera, the architect of El Escorial. The archives were established here by Carlos III in 1785. This sober, Renaissance-style building has two floors with architrave bays. Of particular note inside is the sumptuous 18C pink and black marble staircase. Only the upper floor, with its large rooms topped with elegant vaults, can be visited. It houses a unique collection of priceless documents on the conquest and colonisation of the Americas, as well as the signatures of Columbus, Magellan, Hernán Cortés, Juan Sebastián Elcano and others.

Plaza del Triunfo

Some of Sevilla's most impressive buildings surround this square, in the centre of which stands a "triumph" (triunfo) to the Immaculate Conception. One side is taken up by the Archivo General de Indias, another by the south side of the cathedral, the third by the Alcázar, with the former Hospital del Rey, now the Casa de la Provincia, on the fourth side.

Archivo General de Indias

Imagen © TURISMO ANDALUZ S.A.

Real Alcázar★★★

Entrance through the Puerta del León. ☎ *95 450 23 23.*

This magnificent palace is unusual for a royal residence in that it was the result of several phases of construction from the 10C onwards; as a result it has a variety of architectural styles. All that remains of the 12C Alcázar of the Almohads is the Patio del Yeso and the fortified arches separating the Patio de la Montería from the Patio del León; the rest of the building dates from the Christian period. In the 13C Alfonso X the Wise built the Gothic-style appartments now known as the Salones de Carlos V. The main nucleus of the palace was built by Pedro I the Cruel in 1362. This masterpiece of Mudéjar art was built by masons from Granada, as can be seen in the decoration, highly influenced by the Alhambra, which dates from the same period. Later modifications were made by Juan II, the Catholic Monarchs, Charles V and Felipe II.

Cuarto del Almirante
To the right of the Patio de la Montería. It was in the Admiral's Apartments that Isabel the Catholic founded the Casa de Contratación in 1503. The Sala de Audiencias (Audience Chamber) contains an altarpiece, the **Virgin of the Navigators*** (1531-36), painted by Alejo Fernández.

Sala de la Justicia and Patio del Yeso
To the left of the Patio de la Montería. The Sala de la Justicia (Justice Chamber) was built in the 14C on top of the remains of the former Almohad palace. Note the finely sculpted plasterwork *(yesería)* and the magnificent cupola.

Palacio de Pedro el Cruel★★★
The narrow façade of Pedro the Cruel's Palace is strongly reminiscent of the Patio del Cuarto Dorado in Granada's Alhambra, with its *sebka* decoration, fragile multifoiled arches and a large epigraphic frieze beneath its carved wood overhang.

The palace is laid out around two patios: the Patio de las Doncellas (Court of the Maidens), which was the centre of officialdom, and the smaller proportioned Patio de las Muñecas (Doll's Court), used for private life.

From here, a small hallway to the left leads to the **Patio de las Doncellas**, a rectangular, well-proportioned patio particularly noteworthy for its exquisite *yesería* decoration, which supports a gallery of foliated arches above paired columns, and its magnificent 14C *azulejo* panels. The upper storey, of Italianate design, was added under Charles V.

A number of attractive Mudéjar rooms open onto this patio: the **Salón del techo del Carlos V** *(1)* (Carlos V's Room), the palace's former chapel, with its splendid

Patio de las Doncellas

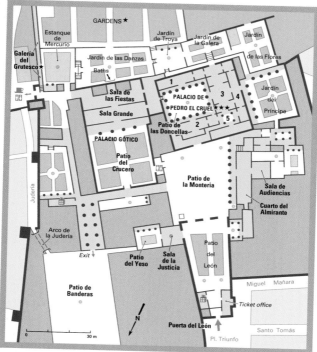

REAL ALCÁZAR

🏛 Shop   🚻 Toilets   ☕ Café

Renaissance ceiling with polygon caissons; the **Dormitorio de los Reyes Moros** *(2)* (Bedroom of the Moorish Kings), two rooms decorated with blue-toned stucco and magnificent *artesonado* ceilings; and the **Salón de Embajadores** *(3)* (Ambassadors' Hall), the most sumptuous room in the Alcázar, with its remarkable 15C half-orange cedarwood **cupola★★★** with stucco decoration. The pendentives have decorative Moorish motifs *(mocárabes)*. The exceptional *azulejo* panelling and the sumptuous wall decoration complete the scene. This room connects with the **Salón del techo de Felipe II** *(4)*, with its magnificent Renaissance coffered cedarwood ceiling.

The Salón de Embajadores leads onto the small-proportioned **Patio de las Muñecas** *(5)*, whose foiled arches, with their

THE CUARTO REAL ALTO

An optional 30min guided tour enables visitors to view the King and Queen of Spain's official residence in Sevilla. The various rooms, with their fine *artesonado* ceilings, contain an impressive display of 19C furniture and clocks, 18C tapestries and French lamps. Of particular note are the **Capilla de los Reyes Católicos** (Chapel of the Catholic Monarchs) – an exquisite oratory with a ceramic font, by Nicola Pisano – and the Mudéjar **Sala de Audiencias**.

Patio de las Doncellas

alfiz surround, clearly demonstrate Granadan influence. The upper floors date from the restoration work carried out in the 19C. This patio opens into the Cuarto del Príncipe (Prince's Room).

Leave the Patio de la Montería and pass through the Corredor de Carlos V, a low-vaulted gallery.

Palacio Gótico or Salones de Carlos V

The Baroque doorway to the Gothic Palace or Charles V's Rooms is to the rear of the **Patio del Crucero**. Built by Alfonso X in Gothic style, it underwent considerable restoration work in the 18C following the Lisbon earthquake. The **Sala Grande**, displaying part of a collection of 17C **tapestries**** from the Real Fábrica de Tapices in Madrid relating the Conquest of Tunis in 1535, dates from this later period. The 13C **Sala de las Fiestas**, or **Sala de las Bóvedas**, is the oldest part of the palace and retains its original structure and groin vaults *(bovédas)* from this era. It was here that Carlos V married Isabel of Portugal. The walls are adorned with attractive 16C *azulejo* panelling and the remainder of the tapestry collection. The large windows provide a foretaste of the palace's enchanting gardens.

Gardens*

The extensive gardens are among the best examples of

this magnificent Moorish art. Like the palace's architecture, they were created over different periods; as a result, Arab, Renaissance and Baroque style are all represented here.

Leave Carlos V's Rooms and pass by the Mercurio Pool to reach the 17C **Galería del Grutesco***, which masks the front of an old wall. The best view of the gardens can be enjoyed from inside this gallery.

To the right, lower down, is the Jardín de las Danzas (Dancing Garden). From here, head to the baths *(baños)* of Doña María de Padilla, a large vaulted pool.

Beyond the **Pabellón de Carlos V**, a 15C pavilion, is the labyrinth, with its clipped hedges. A modern, English-style garden can be seen to the right. A quiet wander through the gardens with just the gentle bubbling of water in the background is an unforgettable experience.

The twin-columned *apeadero*, a covered room in Baroque style, leads to the Patio de Banderas.

Patio de Banderas

The Flag Court, as it is known, was formerly the parade ground *(patio de armas)* of the original Alcázar. This enclosed rectangular square, with its characteristic orange trees and a single fountain, is bordered by elegant façades, against which can be seen the silhouette of the Giralda.

The Mercurio Pool, with the Galeria in the background

Santa Cruz District★★★

This typical quarter, with its delightful narrow, twisting streets, whitewashed houses, flower-filled patios and shady squares is the quintessential *barrio* of Sevilla. In the Middle Ages the Barrio de Santa Cruz was the city's Jewish quarter *(Judería)*. It benefited from royal protection after the Reconquest until the end of the 14C, when increasing intolerance resulted in its seizure and occupation by the Christians, who converted the synagogues into churches.

Today, it is a haven of peace and quiet in the historical heart of Sevilla, where time seems to have stopped. Visitors will want to meander through its alleyways – resplendent in the bright sunshine, and equally delightful at night – and enjoy an unforgettable experience as they discover its many facets and the hospitality of its bars and restaurants, particularly during the *paseo*, when the quarter is imbued with its own inimitable atmosphere.

One of the best entrances to the quarter is through the **Arco de la Judería**, a covered alleyway leading to the Patio de Banderas, transporting the visitor several centuries back in time. Continue to the **callejón del Agua**, which runs alongside the district's outer wall. A less theatrical yet equally interesting route upon leaving the Patio de Banderas is through the **calle Romero Murube**, continuing along the wall of the Alcázar to the plaza de la Alianza. Having crossed the square, follow the street which becomes the twisting yet delightful **callejón de Rodrigo Caro**, ending up at the **plaza de Doña Elvira**, one of Santa Cruz's most typical squares with its *azulejo*-adorned benches shaded by orange trees and its small stone fountain at its centre. The calle Gloria leads to the lively **plaza de los Venerables**, flanked by the hospital of the same name.

Hospital de los Venerables★

☎ 954 56 26 96. Founded in 1675, this hospital for priests, designed by the architect Leonardo de Figueroa, is one of the finest examples of 17C Sevillian Baroque art. It now serves as the headquarters of the FOCUS cultural foundation. Its attractive square patio is decorated with 19C *azulejos*. The **church★**, with its single nave and barrel vault with lunettes, is covered with **frescoes★★** painted by Valdés Leal

---

THE BARBER OF SEVILLE

The city was to provide the inspiration for this comic opera, created in 1816 by the Italian composer Gioacchino Rossini (1792-1868). Written in two acts, this masterpiece tells of the attempts of Bartolo, an elderly doctor, to marry his pretty ward, Rosina. His plans are foiled by another admirer, Count Almaviva, through the help of his acquaintance, Figaro, who also happens to be Bartolo's barber.

DON JUAN

This legendary character, the archetypal seducer who shows no respect for anyone or anything, appears for the first time in Tirso de Molina's *The Trickster of Seville and His Guest of Stone* (1630). It is said that he may have found his inspiration for the character in Don Miguel de Mañara, the founder of the Hospital de la Caridad.

Although the character is known to the world of opera as Mozart's *Don Giovanni* and has been re-created time and time again over the centuries by writers of the stature of Molière, Dumas and Byron, none of whom could resist his attraction, the most well-known version in Spain is that of *Don Juan Tenorio* (1844) by Zorrilla, in whose memory the statue in the plaza de los Refinadores has been erected.

and his son Lucas Valdés. Particularly impressive are *The Last Supper* by Valdés the Younger and, above it, *The Apotheosis of San Fernando*, by Valdés the Elder, both of which are in the apsidal end. The nave contains four Flemish works on copper and two smaller works painted on marble. Two fine statues by Pedro Roldán, *San Fernando* and *San Pedro*, are displayed at the foot of the church. Organ concerts are frequently held in the church, hence the position of the pews.

The **sacristy** contains a fresco by Valdés Leal on the theme of the triumph of the Cross. The balustrade, which appears to change position if you keep watching it as you wander around the room, is also worthy of note. Admire also the anonymous 18C figures of Christ in ivory.

The attractive **main staircase*** is topped by an elliptical Baroque dome adorned with stuccoes bearing the papal coat of arms. Another work by Lucas Valdés, *The Presentation of the Infant Jesus in the Temple*, hangs on the wall.

Streets and squares

Many of the quarter's streets carry evocative names – such as Mesón del Moro (Moor's Inn), Gloria, Pimienta (Pepper) and Susona, from a legend describing the love affair of a disgraced Jewish woman and a Christian man – or have played an important part in the city's history.

By following calle Santa Teresa – look out for n°7, the house in which the artist Murillo lived (now an exhibition room) – or exiting plaza de Alfaro, you come to **plaza de Santa Cruz**, which has lent its name to the quarter. In the middle of the square, amid orange trees, stands an impressive iron cross, the 17C Cruz de la Cerrajería. Here, one of the city's favourite sons, Murillo, is buried. Close by are the gardens which carry his name.

Calle Mezquita leads to the majestic **plaza de los Refinadores** where, in the shade of five palm trees, there stands a statue in honour of Don Juan Tenorio. The **plaza de las Tres Cruces**, a small, triangular square with three columns upon which stand three wrought-iron crosses, is reached via a narrow alleyway.

Calle Mateos Gago, which runs into plaza de la Virgen de los Reyes, has a number of popular bars as well as several early-20C houses. From here, you may wish to enjoy one of the most impressive views of the Giralda. It is difficult to resist the temptation of a few tapas and a beer or *fino* as you take in the delightful surroundings.

Exploring
the city

Palacio De San Telmo and Parque de María Luisa ★

Palacio de San Telmo

This impressively wide palace, built at the end of the 17C, now serves as the headquarters of the Presidencia de la Junta de Andalucía (Regional Parliament). It was formerly a naval academy and then the residence of the Dukes of Montpensier. In the early part of the 20C it became a seminary. Its **main portal★**, one of the finest examples of Sevillian Baroque, is by the architect Leonardo de Figueroa. It is completely covered with a sumptuous decoration of reliefs and sculptures. Above, a statue of San Telmo is silhouetted against the sky.

Hotel Alfonso XIII

The most famous of all Sevilla's hotels was built for the 1929 Ibero-American Exhibition in regionalist style with neo-Mudéjar features, so in vogue at the time and visible in other buildings around the city from the same period.

University

The city's university is housed in a fine building with classical, harmonious lines and impressive dimensions, built in the 18C as Sevilla's tobacco factory. The main façade of this square, two-storey edifice fronting calle San Fernando has an attractive **portal** on two levels with paired columns, crowned by a pediment bearing a large coat of arms, on whose vertex stands an allegorical statue of an angel of the apocalypse representing Fame. The doorway arch bears reliefs and medallions with the busts of Christopher Columbus and Hernán Cortés. The interior is well worth a look, with its attractive patios and monumental staircase. The workers in the old tobacco factory are now firmly entrenched in the city's history thanks to Bizet's *Carmen*.

Parque de María Luisa ★★

The park, one of Sevilla's most popular outdoor areas, was a gift given to the city by the Infanta María Luisa Fernanda, the Duchess of Montpensier, and once formed part of the gardens of the Palacio de San Telmo. The modifications resulting in its present-day appearance were carried out for the 1929 Ibero-American Exhibition by Jean-Claude Nicolas Forestier.

This magnificent, romantic garden with its gazebos, pools and lush and varied vegetation was further enhanced by the buildings erected for the 1929 Exhibition, which have added even more splendour to an already delightful park.

Palacio de San Telmo

Balustrade, Parc María Luisa

Imagen © TURISMO ANDALUZ

Plaza de España* – This magnificent creation, the work of the Sevillian architect Aníbal González, is semicircular in shape and fronted by a canal on which rowing boats can nowadays be hired. The striking features of the *plaza* are its enormous proportions and its exquisite ceramics. In front of the brick building, flanked at either end by two tall towers, are a series of *azulejo* scenes, each one representing a province of Spain and illustrating an episode from its particular history.

Plaza de América – Here we find three buildings by the same architect which were also built for the 1929 Exhibition: at one end the Pabellón Real (Royal Pavilion), in Isabelline style; and opposite, towards the centre, the Renaissance pavilion, now home to the **Museo Arqueológico de Sevilla*** *(see description under "Museums")*, and the Mudéjar pavilion, which houses the **Museo de las Artes y Costumbres Populares** *(see description under "Museums")*.

GAZEBOS, STATUES AND FOUNTAINS

The Parque de María Luisa is much more than just a collection of attractive buildings and long, tree-lined avenues. Its fountains, with their gentle murmuring of water, its gazebos and its statues of famous characters add an intimate, romantic air to this delightful park. The memorials to Gustavo Adolfo Bécquer and Cervantes, with its *azulejos* illustrating scenes from *Don Quixote (at one end of plaza de América)*, are just two examples of the surprises awaiting visitors as they stroll around the gardens

The river bank ★

The **paseo de Cristóbal Colón**, one of Sevilla's most pleasant avenues, runs parallel to the river between the San Telmo and Triana bridges and is lined by some of the city's most impressive sites, such as the Torre del Oro and the Real Maestranza bullring. It offers attractive views across the river to the Triana district on the opposite bank.

Torre del Oro
This splendid tower, along with the Torre de la Plata or Silver Tower, was originally built as part of the city's defensive system. The main part of the tower consists of a dodecago-nal stone structure crowned with merlons, topped by two additional levels in brick, the second of which was added in the 18C. The interior houses the **Museo de la Marina** (☎ 954 22 24 19), containing documents, engravings, models of boats and other items relating to maritime life.

Cruises along the Guadalquivir depart from just below the tower.

Opposite the Torre del Oro stands the **Teatro de la Maestranza**, with its unusual false façade. The Hospital de la Caridad, with its collection of important works of art, is situated just behind the theatre.

Esperanza de Triana, Capilla de los Marineros

Hospital de la Caridad*

The Hospital of Charity was founded in 1667 by Don Miguel de Mañara (1627-79). The whitewashed façade of the church, dazzlingly bright in the sunlight, has five murals of blue and white ceramics apparently based on drawings by Murillo: theological virtues predominate with Faith, Hope and Charity; the two below show St George slaying the dragon and St James (Santiago), the slayer of the Moors *(see description of the tour under "Monuments and sights of interest")*.

Upon leaving the hospital, note the statue of its founder opposite and, to the left, between buildings, the **Torre de la Plata**.
Return to the paseo de Cristóbal Colón and continue towards the Puente de Triana.

La Maestranza

Sevilla's famous *plaza de toros*, with its attractive red and white façade, was built between 1758 and 1881. One interesting feature of the building is the bullring itself, which is not quite circular. The Puerta del Príncipe (Prince's Gate) is an important feature of La Maestranza, for it is through this gate that triumphant bullfighters are carried on the shoulders of their admiring fans. The **museum** (☎ 954 22 45 77) displays an interesting assortment of posters, paintings, busts, bull-fighters' costumes and other mementoes from the world of bullfighting.
Head down to the river.

Just before the Puente de Triana stands the **Monumento a la Tolerancia**, a large stone sculpture with the inimitable stamp of Eduardo Chillida, who spent time here in April 1992.

Triana*

The Triana district, one of the city's most colourful areas, is located on the other side of the Puente de Triana (or Puente de Isabel II), built in 1845. From here, there are fine **views** of the Guadalquivir and the city's major sights on the east bank. By tradition, Triana is a fishermen's and merchants' quarter, although it has also produced several famous singers and bullfighters.

To the left of the bridge, the **plaza del Altozano** has a monument to a famous *trianero* (despite the fact that he was born in calle de la Feria on the opposite bank of the river), namely Juan Belmonte (1892-1962), a key figure in the history of bullfighting.

Enter the Triana district through the **calle Pureza**. At n° 55, between simple yet well-maintained houses, stands the **Capilla de los Marineros**, a chapel dedicated to sailors, with a statue of the **Esperanza de Triana** (Hope of Triana), one of the most venerated statues of the Virgin Mary

CARMEN

This legendary character created by the French writer Prosper Merimée in 1845 was subsequently used by Bizet as the subject of his famous opera (1874), in which he narrates the story of a triangle of love and jealousy involving Carmen the cigar-maker, a soldier and a bullfighter.

Just in front of La Maestranza, in which the tragic finale of the opera was played, a bronze statue has been erected in honour of Carmen, who has gone down in history as the personification of women's passionate love.

Torre del Oro

BARRIO CERAMISTA

A number of ceramics workshops and boutiques can still be seen in the area near the plaza del Altozano occupied by the calle de Callao, calle Antillano and calle de Alfarería, perpetuating an artistic tradition which has always existed in this quarter. The façades of some of these shops and workshops are decorated with *azulejos* advertising the wares inside.

in the city, whose procession rivals that of La Macarena. A Christ of the Three Falls, dating from the end of the 16C, is to the right of the high altar.

Parroquia de Santa Ana

Calle Pureza. A little further on, the Iglesia de Santa Ana in the parish *(parroquía)* of the same name is the oldest in Sevilla. The original church, founded by Alfonso X the Wise in the 13C, has undergone significant restoration and alteration work, most of which took place in the 18C.

Exterior – Because of these various modifications, it is difficult to assign a particular

Imagen © TURISMO ANDALUZ S.A.

style to the church. The most striking feature, however, is the tower, with its multifoiled arches in the lower sections showing clear Mudéjar influence, and its *azulejo* decoration in the upper part.

Interior – *Entrance to the side of the church, in calle Vázquez de Leca.* The interior has three elevated aisles covered with sexpartite vaults and contains a number of paintings and sculptures.

A **Renaissance altarpiece** in the chancel comprises a fine ensemble of sculptures and paintings dedicated to the Virgin Mary; several of the canvases are by Pedro de Cam-

paña. A sculpture portraying St Anne and the Virgin and Child occupies the central vaulted niche. The Child is modern, yet the figures of St Anne and the Virgin date from the 13C, although they have undergone subsequent alteration.

The retro-choir contains the delicate **Virgin of the Rose**, created by Alejo Fernández at the beginning of the 16C. Admire also the panelling and altar, both showing attractive *azulejo* decoration, in a chapel in the Evangelist nave.

Calle Betis

This street runs alongside the river. It is well worth taking the time to stroll along it, enjoying the delightful views of the opposite bank which provide the visitor with a completely different perspective of Sevilla, with the Torre del Oro and La Maestranza in the foreground, dominated by the majestic outline of the Giralda. The street is also noteworthy for its houses, bars and open-air kiosks which combine to create a scene which has managed to retain its traditional charm. At night, with the moon reflected on the river, the street is the perfect place for a romantic stroll.

"EL CACHORRO"

The **Capilla del Patrocinio**, a chapel situated at the end of the calle Castilla in the most northerly section of the Triana district, is where the **Christ of the Expiration,** commonly known as "El Cachorro", is venerated. It is said that the artist, Francisco Antonio Gijón, used a sketch of a murdered gypsy known as "El Cachorro" for the face of Christ in this late-17C masterpiece. Once he had finished carving Christ, the sculpture was so realistic that when people saw it they immediately recognised the dead gypsy, hence its name.

La Maestranza

La Macarena and calle San Luis *

Basilíca de la Macarena
☎ 954 90 18 00. The Iglesia de Nuestra Señora de la Esperanza (Church of Our Lady of Hope), built in the middle of the 20C, contains one of Sevilla's most famous statues: **La Macarena***. This carving of the Virgin Mary, the work of an anonymous 17C artist, looks down upon the church from the high altar. The city's inhabitants say that it was sculpted by the angels, as only they could have created a work of such magnificence. The beauty of her tearful face unleashes popular fervour during her procession, in the early morning of Good Friday. A Christ under Sentence in a chapel on the Evangelist side of the church is also venerated here and brought out in the procession alongside the Virgin.

The **museum** displays a variety of cloaks and skirts, as well as the impressive floats used to carry La Macarena and Christ during the processions, providing the visitor with an idea of the splendour of these occasions.

The **Arco de la Macarena** stands opposite the church. This arch was part of the old Arab **walls** of the city. The section which has been preserved continues as far as the Puerta de Córdoba (Córdoba Gate). The walls have barbicans and are punctuated with large, square fortified towers.

Hospital de las Cinco Llagas or Hospital de la Sangre
Opposite the Arco de la Macarena. The former Hospital of the Five Wounds (*llagas*) or Blood (*sangre*), is now the headquarters of the Andalusian Parliament. Up until the middle of the 20C, this Renaissance-style building was Sevilla's main hospital. It is sober and harmonious in style with two floors opening out onto a square of greenery, and has towers on each corner. The building's white marble doorway is crowned by the escutcheon of the Five Wounds.

Return to La Macarena, behind which stands the 13C parish church of **San Gil**, which has undergone significant restoration over the centuries. Follow the calle de San Luis.

Iglesia de Santa Marina
This 14C brick church has a simple stone ogival portal with minor sculpted decoration and a sober Mudéjar tower with staggered merlons. A tour of the exterior reveals the church's sturdy buttresses and the large Gothic windows at the apsidal end.

Iglesia de San Luis de los Franceses *
This church, the work of Leonardo de Figueroa, is one of the best examples of Sevillian Baroque architecture. The

predominant feature of the façade is its clear compartmentalisation: two storeys, with an octagonal tower on each side, between which stands a central cupola with ceramic decoration.

The **interior**** is surprising in its exuberant beauty, with murals on the magnificent cupola by Lucas Valdés and the outstanding retables by Pedro Duque Cornejo. The fine *azulejos* complete this superb ensemble, which manages to combine a richness of decoration with harmony. Note also the unusual reliquary on the frontal of the chancel.

Iglesia de San Marcos

The impressive 14C façade is a successful blend of Gothic and Mudéjar features. The

G. Bludzin/MICHELIN

Andalusian Parliament, formerly the Hospital of the Five Wounds

PARLAMENTO
DE ANDALVCIA

Andalusian Parliament

Imagen © TURISMO ANDALUZ S.

attractive **Mudéjar tower*** stands out, with its clear Giralda influence (multifoiled arches and *sebka* work on the upper frieze). The predominant building material is brick, with the exception of the stone portal which is Gothic in style and has three 18C sculptures (God the Father, the Virgin Mary and an angel), which replaced the original works, and an elegant *sebka*-style frieze lending it an unusual air.

The whitewashed interior contains a handsome 17C sculpture of **St Mark** (Evangelist nave) and an 18C **Recumbent Christ** (Epistle nave).

In the **plaza de Santa Isabel** behind the church, admire the doorway of the **convent** that has lent its name to the square, with a relief depicting the Visitation of the Virgin to her cousin Elizabeth. The work dates from the early 17C and is by Andrés Ocampo. The church is interesting, albeit somewhat difficult to visit as it only opens for daily mass first thing in the morning.

A little further along stands the **Convento de Santa Paula***, one of the most ornate convents in the city *(see description under "Monuments and sights of interest")*.

Centro district ★

Plaza Nueva

This spacious, rectangular square is situated on the land previously occupied by the Convento de San Francisco. An equestrian statue at its centre is of Fernando III the Saint, the city's conqueror. With its tall palm trees, benches and street lamps, the square is popular with locals and tourists alike.

Ayuntamiento

The west front of the town hall, which opens onto the square, is neo-Classical and dates from the 19C. The more interesting east side, which looks onto the plaza de San Francisco, has an attractive 16C **façade★** which is pure Plateresque in style and is the work of Diego de Riaño. The delicate decoration (a mixture of classical ornamental motifs including fantastic and grotesque animals, medallions with faces, escutcheons etc) can be seen on the architraves, columns, pilasters and bay surrounds.

The attractive palace situated opposite the town hall in plaza de San Francisco is the headquarters of the Caja de Ahorros San Fernando savings bank and was formerly the seat of the Royal Court of Justice (*Audiencia*). The classical lines of its late-16C façade are attributed to Alonso de Vandelvira.

J. Bouraly/MICHELIN

Town hall

Calle Sierpes

This long pedestrianised street, undoubtedly the most famous in the city, is lined with a whole host of shops, both traditional and modern. Sierpes is at its most lively in the late afternoon and early evening when locals stroll along the street window-shopping or enjoy a pastry in one of its renowned *pastelerías*. When the sun is at its hottest, a protective canopy is used along the whole street to provide protection and coolness for those still out and about. The famous La Campana cafeteria and pastry shop, founded in 1885, is located at the very end of calle Sierpes, at the junction with calle Martín Villa.

Capilla de San José*

This exquisite chapel, built at the end of the 17C, is a masterpiece of Sevillian Baroque. Its 18C façade and belfry decorated with bright blue *azulejos* can be seen from the corner of calle Sierpes and calle Jovellanos. St Joseph with the Infant Christ in his arms can be seen on the portal. The exuberant Baroque decoration in the relatively small interior is something of a surprise, particularly that visible in the apsidal end. The large wooden **altarpiece** in the presbytery depicting angels, saints and God the Father, is a true apotheosis of ornamental art. The image of St Joseph in the centre of the altarpiece is venerated here.

At the end of calle Sierpes, take calle Cuna, which runs parallel to it.

The most impressive building along this street is the magnificent **Palacio de la Condesa de Lebrija*** *(see description under "Monuments and sights of interest").*

Continue along calle Cuna to plaza del Salvador.

Plaza del Salvador

This spacious, elongated square is dominated by the monumental parish church of El Salvador. The plaza is one of the city's most popular places for an aperitif, when it swaps its customary peace and quiet for a few hours of lively socialising, especially on Sundays.

Iglesia del Salvador* – The church rises majestically on one side of the square. It was built on the site of the former main mosque, which was demolished in 1671. Construction work lasted until 1712, in accordance with plans by José Granados; the cupolas were designed by Leonardo de Figueroa. The elegant façade of the church, which combines attractive pink brick and stone, is a fine example of the ornamental Baroque style.

The sensation of vastness pervades the whole of the interior. The spacious church has a ground plan consisting of three short aisles. Note the high lanterned cupola above the transept.

Some of the city's most notable **Baroque retables**** (all of which date from the 18C) can be seen inside the church. The one in the chancel, dedicated to the Transfiguration of the Lord, is the work of Cayetano Acosta. This immense altarpiece covers the entire wall with unrestrained decoration that completely masks its artistic arrangement.

The frontispiece of the **Capilla del Sagrario**, the sacrarium chapel which opens onto the left transept, has been designed in the form of a gigantic retable. This is also the work of Cayetano Acosta, and is dedicated to the exaltation of the Sacred Host; it displays the same ornamental exuberance as the main altarpiece. Inside the chapel, the most interesting object is the 17C **Christ of the Passion**, by Martínez Montañés. This work, which is part of an opulent silver altarpiece, manages to create an image of serene suffering in the face of Christ. Another fine retable, by José Maestre, with a shrine dedicated to the Virgin Mary, can be admired in the right transept.

The chapel to the right of the chancel displays the 17C **Crucificado del Amor**, by Juan de Mesa, in which the artist movingly interprets the suffering and solitude of Jesus on the Cross.

Calle Sierpes

From plaza del Duque de la Victoria to Alameda de Hercules

Plaza del Duque de la Victoria is the commercial heart of this part of the city with several department stores and numerous smaller shops.

In the nearby **plaza de la Concordia**, Sevilla's town hall has created an exhibition centre in the church of the former Colegio de San Hermenegildo (1616-20), which has preserved its fine oval cupola.

Walk through plaza de Gavidia, with its statue of Daoíz, then take calle Cardenal Spínola, which leads into plaza de San Lorenzo.

Templo de Nuestro Padre Jesús del Gran Poder

This modern church (1965), housing the magnificent statue of **Jesus of Great Power*** (1620), is situated in plaza de San Lorenzo, alongside the parish church of the same name dating from the 13C but modified four centuries later. Juan de Mesa's sculptural masterpiece is housed in a shrine surrounded by red carnations, where the devout come to leave their offerings.

The slightly inclined face of Jesus reflects with realism his great fatigue and profound sadness.

Follow calle Santa Clara, along which the convent of the same name, an enclosed order of nuns, can be seen (but not visited), and then head along calle Lumbreras. Once past the junction with calle Becas, turn around to admire the **Torre de Don Fadrique**, all that remains of the Palacio de Don Fadrique. This battlemented tower was built in the 13C in a transitional style showing both Romanesque and Gothic influence.

Continue along calle Lumbreras as far as Alameda de Hércules.

Alameda de Hércules

This long boulevard was constructed in the 16C. Two statues stand at each end: those to the north were added in the 18C and show two lions bearing coats of arms; those to the south are Roman and are crowned by statues of Hercules and Julius Caesar. A **flea market** provides a lively atmosphere here on Sunday mornings.

Museums

Museo de Bellas Artes★★★

This excellent art gallery contains one of the largest collections of Spanish paintings from the Golden Age. It is housed in the former Convento de la Merced (17C), designed by Juan de Oviedo; the Baroque doorway was added in the 18C. The museum is built around three delightful patios and a magnificent staircase, covered by a cupola decorated with Mannerist stucco designs.

The gallery displays a number of significant works from the Middle Ages to the 20C. However, two rooms are of particular importance:

Visit

Entrance via the plaza del Museo. ☎ *954 22 07 90.*

Room V★★★ – *Ground floor.* This is undoubtedly the star attraction. The church, its walls decorated with paintings by the 18C artist Domingo Martínez, provides a stunning backdrop to an outstanding collection of work by Murillo and one of Zurbarán's masterpieces, *The Apotheosis of St Thomas Aquinas (in the nave).* **Murillo** (1617-82), a master of both the pictorial technique and the use of light in his canvases, is the great painter of religious subjects and children. His characters, always very human, exude tenderness and gentleness in a world which avoids drama

and excess. His canvases can be found in the transept and in the apse, where his monumental *Immaculate Conception,* with its energetic movement, holds pride of place. It is surrounded by several notable paintings of saints: *Santa Rufina and Santa Justa,* who are clutching the Giralda, and *San Leandro and San Buenaventura.* In the right transept, a kindly *Virgin of the Cloth* is particularly interesting (admire the effect of the child moving towards you). Note also *St Francis embracing Christ on the Cross* and a further *Immaculate Conception,* also known as *La Niña (The Child).* Among several paintings on the left-hand side, *St Anthony and Child, Dolorosa* and *St Felix of Cantalicio and Child* are all worth a closer look.

Room X★★ – *Upper floor.* This room is dedicated to works by **Francisco de Zurbarán** (1598-1664). This artist had a particular skill for painting the shades of white of the monks' habits and the pure cloth of Christ, as admired in the fine *Christ on the Cross* (in this same room), in which the body of Christ, painted against a dark background, appears as if sculpted in relief. Zurbarán's compositions are both simple and peaceful. A certain lack of concern for perspective is apparent in some of his work, resulting in one or two inac-

Maculate Conception by Murillo in the Museo de Bellas Artes

curacies, as can be seen in *St Hugh and Carthusian Monks at Table* which is otherwise quite outstanding. His preoccupation with the treatment of the canvas, as already seen in his depiction of the Fathers of the Church in *The Apotheosis of St Thomas Aquinas*, can equally be admired in the splendid velvet brocade in *San Ambrosio*. In addition to his paintings of saints, his *Virgin of the Caves* and *San Bruno's Visit to Urbano II* are also of interest. On display in the same room are various sculptures, including *St Dominic* by Martínez Montañés. Note also the splendid *artesonado* ceiling in the inner room.

Other rooms – Room I displays a number of interesting medieval works. **Room II**, once the refectory, is dedicated to Renaissance art, in particular a fine sculpture of *St Jerome* by Pietro Torrigiani, a contemporary of Michelangelo. Other works of note include Alejo Fernández's *Annunciation*, with its Flemish and Italian influence clearly evident, a painting of his son *Jorge Manuel*, by El Greco, and a diptych of *The Annunciation*

and Visitation by Coffermans. Two magnificent portraits of *A Lady and a Gentleman* by Pedro Pacheco are the highlights in **Room III**.

Upper floor: **Room VI** (a gallery) displays a fine, richly decorated collection of female saints (anonymous, though some were painted by followers of Zurbarán), and two male saints. **Room VII** contains further works by Murillo and his disciples while **Room VIII** is entirely devoted to the other great Baroque artist **Valdés Leal**, a more expressive and dramatic painter than Murillo. European Baroque is represented in **Room IX** by, among others, Ribera's powerful *St James the Apostle*, canvases by Brueghel and the supreme *Portrait of a Lady* by Cornelis de Vos. **Room XI** (a gallery), devoted to 18C art, is enlivened by Goya's *Portrait of Canon José Duato*, and several works by Lucas Valdés. The following two rooms (**XII** and **XIII**) display 19C art, in particular some superb portraits by Esquivel, while the final room (**XIV**) shows several 20C canvases by Vázquez Díaz and Zuloaga, among others.

La Cartuja-Centro Andaluz de Arte Contemporáneo

The Andalusian Centre for Contemporary Art is in the former monastery of La Cartuja, and is part of an unusual complex with a complicated history.

Local buses C-1 and C-2.
☏ *955 03 70 70.*

The monastery was founded at the end of the 14C in honour of an apparition of the Virgin Mary in this district. It subsequently enjoyed a period of great splendour and even visits by kings and queens and other important figures such as Columbus, who prepared his second journey of discovery to America here. During the 19C, the monastery was to undergo significant changes: the French converted it into a barracks during the Napoleonic invasion and it was later acquired by Charles Pickman, who set up a ceramics factory on the site. Although the factory closed in 1982, its chimneys and kilns are still visible today.

Monastic buildings★ – These mainly date from the 15C, 16C and 17C. Some have managed to preserve their original *azulejos*. The church is of particular interest with its delightful *azulejo* rosette, a sacristy with Baroque plasterwork and charming Mudéjar brick cloisters supported by slender marble columns. The monks' chapter house, containing a number of interesting tombs, and the long refectory with a superb 17C *artesonado* ceiling, are also well worth a visit.

Museum – The museum's collection mainly comprises early-20C works by major names such as Miró and Chillida, as well as those by young Andalusian contemporary artists. The centre also hosts regular temporary exhibitions.
☏ *954 23 24 01.*

Museo Arqueológico de Sevilla ★

Housed in a Renaissance pavilion in plaza de América, within the confines of the Parque María Luisa, the city's archaeological museum contains an interesting collection of prehistoric and Roman objects.

Visit

☎ 954 23 24 01.

The prehistoric collection is displayed on the ground floor, and includes items discovered at archaeological excavations carried out around the province. The exhibits in **Room VI** are particularly exciting, comprising the 7C-6C BC **El Carambolo treasure★**, a superb collection of gold jewellery of Phoenician inspiration with a surprisingly modern design, and the **Goddess Astarte** (8C BC), a small bronze statue bearing an inscription which is said to be the oldest script found on the Iberian peninsula.

The first floor is dedicated exclusively to the museum's **Roman collection★** (Rooms XII to XXV), the majority of which was discovered at Itálica. Exhibits include magnificent sculptures and mosaics which provide visitors with an insight into the artistic development of the Romans in the region. Other displays show a variety of objects which re-create various aspects of the Roman civilisation (domestic life, religion, commerce, coins etc).

Other items of interest in the museum include a Mercury with a large mosaic at his feet (Room XIV); an unusual collection of marble plaques with footprint markings offered at games ceremonies (Room XVI); a Venus in Room XVII; fine sculptures of Diana in Room XIX; and bronze plaques from the Roman Lex Irnitana in the annexe. The oval room (Room XX) contains an impressive statue of Trajan, while Room XXV, dedicated to funerary art, has a variety of sarcophagi, columbaria, household objects etc.

Museo de las Artes y Costumbres Populares

☎ *954 23 25 76. Opposite the archaeological museum.* Within the Mudéjar pavilion, the Museum of Popular Art and Traditions displays a range of ethnographic exhibits such as traditional costumes worn for *romerías* and *fiestas*, a reconstruction of typical workshop scenes, musical instruments, farming tools and machinery, as well as a collection of posters for the April Fair.

Diana, Museo Arqueológico

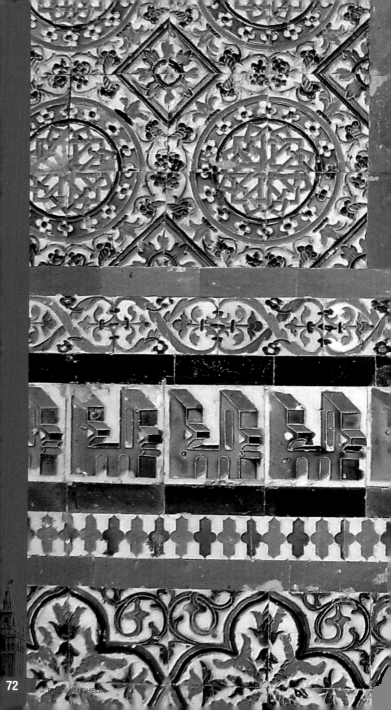

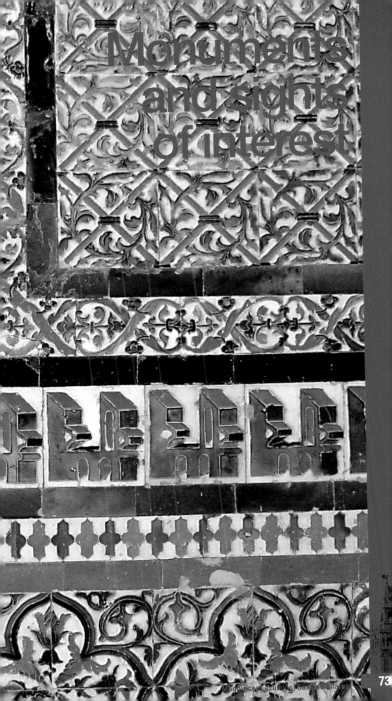

Monuments and sights of interest

Magníficos azulejos, Casa de Pilatos

Casa de Pilatos **

The palace is one of Sevilla's most famous monuments. It is situated in the pleasant **plaza de Pilatos** to which it has lent its name. The statue in the square is of Zurbarán.

Visit

☎ 954 22 52 98.

Construction of the building began at the end of the 15C. However, it was Don Fadrique, the first Marquess of Tarifa, who was responsible for most of the palace visible today. It is said that he took his inspiration from Pontius Pilate's house in Jerusalem, hence the name of the palace. It is a mixture of Mudéjar, Renaissance and Flamboyant Gothic styles, although the Mudéjar style predominates.

The delightful **patio** resembles an elegant Moorish palace with its finely moulded stuccowork and magnificent 16C lustre **azulejos****. Note that the arches are unequal and that the *azulejos* form panels that have different motifs. A fountain in the centre was carved in Genoa in the 16C. Various statues decorate the palace, including **Athena**, an original 5C BC Greek statue; the remaining statues are of Roman origin. Rounded niches in the walls contain a superb collection of busts of Roman emperors. The rooms around the patio are noteworthy for their fine *artesonado* ceilings, panels of *azulejos*, sculpted plasterwork, groined vaulting and the palaeo-Christian sculpture of the Good Shepherd in the chapel, the oldest part of the house. The gardens can also be visited.

The sumptuous *azulejo*-adorned **staircase**** leading up to the first floor from a corner of the patio has a remarkable half-orange **wooden dome***.

Frescoes from the 16C representing various characters from Antiquity can be seen on the walls of the patio gallery on this upper floor. Several of the rooms have interesting ceilings, particularly the one painted by Francisco Pacheco in 1603 illustrating the Apotheosis of Hercules.

A visit to the nearby **Convento de San Leandro** is particularly recommended. Although access to the church is difficult, it is still worth a visit to buy the convent's famous **yemas**, delicious sweets made with egg yolk and sugar.

Gardens, Casa de Pilatos

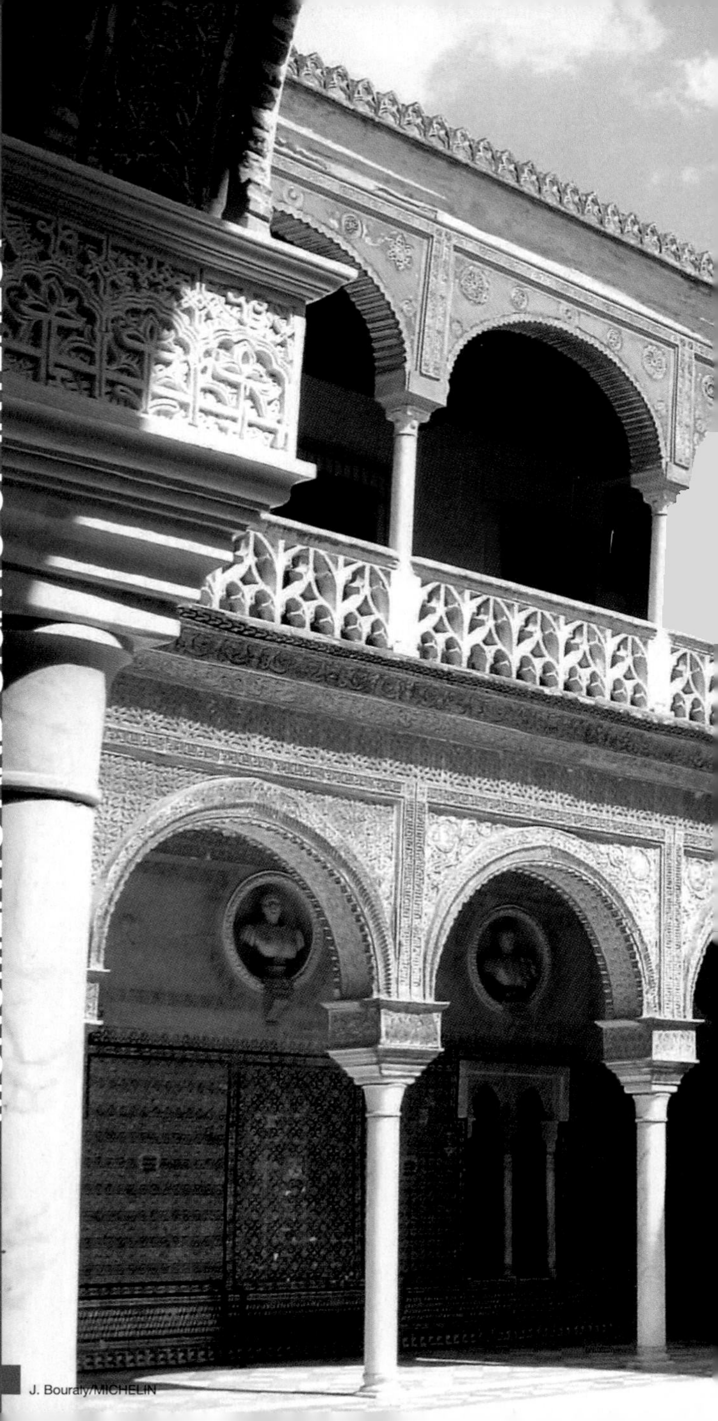

J. Bourajy/MICHELIN

Delightful patio of the Casa de Pilatos

Hospital de la Caridad ★

The Hospital of Charity was founded in 1667 by Don Miguel de Mañara (1627-79). The whitewashed façade of the church, dazzlingly bright in the sunlight, has five murals of blue and white ceramics apparently based on drawings by Murillo: theological virtues predominate with Faith, Hope and Charity; the two below show St George slaying the dragon and St James (Santiago), the slayer of the Moors.

The entrance to the church is via the hospital, with its harmonious double patio adorned with panels of *azulejos* representing scenes from the Old and New Testaments.

Visit
☎ 954 22 32 32.

Church★★ – The single-nave Baroque church contains a number of artistic gems within its walls commissioned by Mañara from Sevilla's leading artists of the period. The pictorial representations of Death and Charity would have created an example of the path that the brothers of Charity were expected to follow.

Two **paintings★★** by **Valdés Leal** beneath the chancel tribune are quite staggering in their severity. In *Finis Gloriae Mundi*, with its macabre realism, Valdés Leal depicts a scene in which a bishop and a knight are shown as dead and half decomposed; the scales held in the hand of Christ are a reference to the moment of judgement. *In Ictu Oculi* (In the Blink of an Eye) is an allegory of death in which the skeleton has earthly symbols at its feet (a globe, a crown, books etc). An *Exaltation of the Cross*, by the same artist, can be seen above the choir.

In the nave, **Murillo** has illustrated the theme of Charity through several **works★**. The sense of submission to one's fellow man is exalted in the fine *St Isabel of Hungary Curing the Lepers*, and in *St John of God Carrying a Sick Man On His Shoulder*, in which the artist demonstrates his mastery of *chiaroscuro*. The two paintings of children on the side altars are also by Murillo. Another side altar has a 17C bleeding Christ casting a distressed gaze toward the sky, by Pedro Roldán. The two horizontal paintings facing each other in the transept are *The Miracle of the Loaves and Fishes* (representing the giving of food to the hungry) and *Moses Smiting Water from the Rock* (representing the giving of water to the thirsty). The canvases in the dome of the transept are by Valdés Leal: in each echinus an angel bearing the instruments of the Passion can be seen; the Evangelists are depicted in the pendentives. Note also the fine lamp-bearing angels.

At the main altar, a splendid Baroque **altarpiece** by Pedro Roldán has at its centre a fine sculptural group representing the **Holy Burial of Christ**★★ in which the artist has interpreted with great beauty the pain in the contained emotion of the faces.

Façade of the hospital church

Convento de Santa Paula★

This historic convent, home to an order of enclosed nuns, was founded at the end of the 15C and is one of the finest in Sevilla. The elegant 17C belfry, which stands proudly above the surrounding houses, acts as an invitation to discover this delightful convent which also produces its own tasty cakes and jams prepared by its Hieronymite nuns.

Visit

☎ 954 53 63 30.

Church★ – *Entrance through the left-hand door with the* azulejo *depicting St Paula.* Once through the door, note the interesting atrium and the fine **portal★** of the church, worked on by Nicola Pisano and completed in 1504. The portal is made of brick with alternating twin-coloured rows and is adorned with profuse ceramic decoration. In spite of the evident mixture of styles – Mudéjar in the use of brick, Gothic in the arches, and Renaissance in the medallions and cresting – the effect is one of perfect cohesion and harmony. The escutcheon on the tympanum is of the Catholic Monarchs. The

B. Kaufmann/MICHELIN

central medallion, attributed to Luca della Robbia, represents the Birth of Jesus.

The **interior***, with a single nave topped by a 17C *artesonado* ceiling, comprises a presbytery with Gothic vaults which are totally covered with delightful polychrome frescoes. The two niches on either side of the high altar contain the tombs of the Marquess and Marchioness of Montemayor, the benefactors of this church. The brother of the Marchioness is laid to rest in a separate niche. The main altarpiece dates from the beginning of the 18C, although it has retained the image of St Paula, in the centre, from an earlier retable. Note the movement of the two lamp-bearing angels. Two altars can be seen in the nave, one opposite the other, dedicated to John the Evangelist and John the Baptist. The two finely carved sculptures are the work of Martínez Montañés. A Gothic Christ can also be seen in a large window in the Epistle nave. The enclosed choir is separated from the rest of the church by an iron grille.

Museo* – *Entrance through n° 11 on the square.* The museum is housed in several of the convent's high outbuildings. Two of these have fine *artesonado* ceilings. The museum contains a number of objects of great value, including canvases by **Ribera** (*St Jerome* and *The Adoration of the Shepherds*), two works by Pedro de Mena (*Our Lady of Sorrows* and *Ecce Homo*), an *Immaculate Conception* by Alonso Cano, and a charming 17C crib with many figurines.

Presbytery vault, Iglesia del Convento de Santa Paula

Isla Mágica Theme Park ★

The Isla Mágica theme park, spread over a 40ha/ 99-acre site on the island of La Cartuja, takes visitors on a journey back to the century of the Discoveries. The park is divided into eight areas: Sevilla, the Gateway to the Indies; Quetzal, the Fury of the Gods; The Balcony of the Gods; The Gateway to America; Amazonia; The Pirates' Den; The Fountain of Youth; and El Dorado.

The park has a whole host of other facilities and attractions, including exciting rides, street entertainers and souvenir shops, as well as a good selection of bars and restaurants where you can catch your breath.

The following is a list of some of the theme park's most popular attractions:

Quetzal, the Fury of the Gods – An exciting journey to the Mayan world in which a plumed serpent takes you on a journey across Central America to escape the fury of the gods.

The Balcony of Andalucía – An enjoyable stroll through this miniature world highlighting the most important monuments and geographical features of the region.

Anaconda – A breathtaking water ride with spectacular descents to satisfy the most intrepid of sailors.

Iguaçu – These impressive waterfalls are bound to get your nerves tingling as you are propelled into a lagoon at speeds of over 50kph/ 32mph.

The Jaguar – If you still need an extra rush of adrenaline, the Jaguar is for you. This huge roller coaster with its loop-the-loops and vertigo-inducing descents reaches speed of up to 85kph/53mph.

The Fountain of Youth – A paradise for **younger visitors**. This dream-like world of lakes and streams contains most of the park's attractions for young children, including the **Tell-Tale Toad** and the **Tadpoles** with their wonderfully amusing stories.

The Rapids of the Orinoco – Why not try your hand at taming this spectacular river on board an inflatable raft.

The House of Superstition – A film created by state-of-the-art technology projected onto a gigantic spherical screen. Experience a whole new world of sensations in the House of Superstition.

Information: ☎ *902 16 17 16; www.islamagica.es – Reservations:* ☎ *902 16 00 00*
Open 2 Apr-1 Nov. Open daily, May to mid-Sep; otherwise, Sat-Sun and on special occasions
(contact the park for further details).

Other places of interest

Palacio de la Condesa de Lebrija*

☎ *954 22 78 02.* This private residence provides visitors with an opportunity to visit a palace with a typically Sevillian layout, comprising a hallway, a central patio and an interior garden. However, once inside, a pleasant surprise awaits – a floor that appears to be completely covered with **Roman mosaics*** from nearby Itálica. Although all the mosaics are of interest, the patio floor depicting mythological scenes is particularly fine, as is the octagonal room with its volutes and large vases. In addition to

12.com/Oronoz

Iglesia Santa Maria la Blanca

the mosaics, the attractive patio also has elegant foiled arches, Moorish-influenced panelling and *alfiz* rectangular moulding, a colourful plinth of Sevillian *azulejos* and showcases displaying archaeological remains. The **staircase***, rich in ceramic tiles, has a mahogany banister, marble steps and an outstanding Mudéjar marquetry ceiling, which originally graced a palace in Marchena.

The rooms and galleries on the upper floor are embellished with a mix of Renaissance, Baroque and romantic decorative features.

Iglesia de Santa María la Blanca*

This former synagogue was transformed into a church in the 14C; the simple Gothic portal remains from this period. However, the 17C saw the almost total reconstruction of the building, including the remainder of the façade and the **interior***. The latter has three aisles separated by semicircular arches resting on pink marble columns. The barrel vaults adorned with lunettes and the dome over the transept are completely covered with delightful plasterwork decoration. The building's Baroque exuberance is balanced by the lightness of the columns, creating an effect which is both attractive and harmonious. The Evangelist nave contains a *Last Supper*, attributed to Murillo, which is surprising in its dramatic use of light, in keeping with the pure tenebrist style.

Iglesia de la Magdalena

The church was built in the late 17C and early 18C on the site of an earlier building, accord-

ing to designs by Leonardo de Figueroa. It is possible to see the layout of the church from the exterior, with its aisles, transept and elegant dome ornamented with *azulejos*.

The **interior***, containing a number of treasures, is particularly impressive. The paintings on the ceilings are the work of Lucas Valdés. A lanterned cupola rises majestically above the transept, while the exuberant Baroque altarpiece in the chancel dates from the early 18C; the paintings on the vaults illustrate allegories of saints. The **Capilla del Cristo del Calvario** *(to the right of the presbytery)* takes its name from *The Exposed Christ*, an 18C work by Francisco Ocampo. Interest in the Epistle nave is centred on the fine **high-relief of the Assumption** supported by four small angels, by Juan de Mesa (1619), and the Sacramental and Quinta Angustia chapels. The former contains two canvases by **Zurbarán**: *St Dominic in Soria* and *The Miraculous Healing of the Beatified Reginald of Orleans*.

The **Capilla de la Quinta Angustia*** is situated in the vestibule of the main entrance doorway to the church. The magnificent sculpture at the altar, depicting a highly moving Deposition, is attributed to the followers of Pedro Roldán. Look up to admire the three Moorish-influenced cupolas. Ten canvases of saints by Valdés Leal hang on the walls of the chapel.

In the left transept, next to the door, stands a 16C sculpture of the **Virgin of the Fever**, an elegant and maternal Virgin with the Infant Christ in her arms.

Aerial view of the city

J. Bouraly/MICHELIN

Excursions

Outskirts of Sevilla

Itálica★

9km/5.5mi NW along the E 803 – N 630. Bear left immediately after Santiponce. ☎ *955 99 73 76/ 65 83.* The history of this Roman city is linked to that of the emperors **Trajan** (AD 53-117) and **Hadrian** (AD 76-138), both of whom were born here. Hadrian granted it the title of a colony, transforming Itálica into a monumental city. Its decline began under the Late Empire. The archaeological area corresponds to a section of the district created under Hadrian, with streets laid out according to an orthogonal plan and lined by public buildings and luxurious private houses. Several original **mosaics** have been preserved, such as those of Neptune, birds, planetary divinities etc. **Amphitheatre** – This elliptical amphitheatre was one of the largest in the Roman Empire with a capacity for 25 000 spectators and is relatively well preserved. Sections of tiered seating and the pits beneath the arena can still be seen.

Roman amphitheatre, Itálica

Imagen © TURISMO ANDALUZ S

The town of **Santiponce** stands on the oldest part of Itálica. The former Roman theatre can be seen at its centre.

Bollullos de la Mitación

18km/11mi W of Sevilla. Leave the city along the A 49 (towards Huelva), turning off at exit 5.

Iglesia de San Martín – Plaza de Cuatrovitas is fronted by the town hall and the Church of St Martin, a Baroque construction dating from the 18C. The brick tower has detailed *azulejo* decoration. Inside, note the interesting **retable** with four paintings by Zurbarán.

Santuario de Cuatrovitas – *Leave Bollullos in the direction of Aznalcázar. After 4km/2.5mi, bear left immediately after a pine grove. Continue for a further 2km/1.2mi along an unmetalled road.*

The drive to this simple sanctuary, one of few rural mosques still standing, is particularly pleasant. Built during the Almohad period in a flat landscape, its most striking features are its brick **tower** and foliated and horseshoe arch decoration. The interior contains a 16C ceramic altar frontispiece representing the Virgin and Child and the Four Evangelists.

Alcalá de Guadaira

20km/12mi SE of Sevilla along the A 92. Drive into the town and park next to the Iglesia de Santiago.

Iglesia de Santiago – The Church of St James was built in the 15C and 16C. Elegant ceramic decoration covers the upper sections and the spire of the lofty bell tower. Inside, note the presbytery, crowned with an unusual trumpet-shaped and coffered vault.

Castle – *Climb up the stepped ramps next to the church.* The remains of this important Almohad fortress stand on top of a hill, dominating the town and an extensive rolling landscape. The walls and towers of the original outer enclosure can still be seen. This pleasant site has now been transformed into a leisure area with a children's park, goalposts etc. The 14C-16C **Ermita de Nuestra Señora del Aguila**, a chapel with a solid brick tower topped by merlons, stands at its centre. Note the remains of a medieval fresco inside the chapel *(to the right of the presbytery).*

Carmona★★

38km/24mi E of Sevilla along the A 4. Population: 25 326. Carmona enjoys an impressive location on a plateau overlooking an expansive fertile plain irrigated by the River Corbones.
🛈 *Alcázar de la Puerta de Sevilla,* ☎ *954 19 09 55.*

Carmona, one of Andalucía's oldest towns, was initially founded by the Carthaginians, and later developed into an important municipality which played an active political role during the period of Roman occupation. The town retained its influence under the Moors, and later, following its reconquest, under the Christians. Vestiges of Carmona's past are clearly visible in its old quarter *(casco antiguo)*, an area of monumental buildings, elegant palaces, seigniorial houses and solemn places of worship.

Old Quarter★
Allow half a day
Leave your car in the lower part of town, near the Puerta de Sevilla.
Walls – The double Moorish-arched **Puerta de Sevilla★** is one of the few remains from the old lower fortress *(alcázar de abajo)*, which served as an entrance to the old quarter. Vestiges of the impressive walls built by the Carthaginians and strengthened by the Romans can also be seen dotted around this district. One of the most impressive features of the old town is the **Puerta de Córdoba★**, where two superb octagonal towers of Roman origin and a gateway added in the 17C can be admired.

Iglesia de San Pedro★ – The Church of St Peter stands along the paseo del Estatuto. This 15C building, which was heavily restored during the Baroque period, has a fine **bell tower★**, similar to the Giralda in Sevilla, from which it has taken the name of "Giraldilla". The most interesting features inside the church are the **Capilla del Sagrario**, the sacrarium chapel with its rich decorative detail, and an extraordinary 16C green ceramic **baptismal font**.

Convento de la Concepción – The convent contains charming **cloisters** and a Mudéjar-style church.
Walk through the Puerta de Sevilla.

Iglesia de San Bartolomé – This church of Gothic origin, rebuilt in the 17C and 18C, has a basilical ground plan and a graceful neo-Classical tower. The interior contains an interesting chapel

Festivals
The town's **Carnival** is renowned throughout the province, as is its famous **Holy Week**, an opportunity to admire the magnificent processions that wind their way through the tranquil narrow streets of the old quarter..

Bell-tower of the Iglesia de San Pedro, known as "Giraldilla"

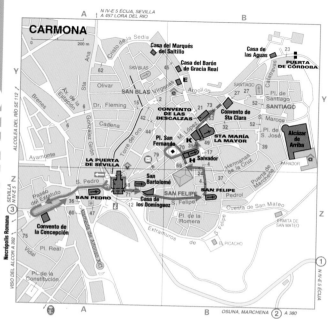

CARMONA

EXCURSIONS

covered with Renaissance *azulejos* (to the left of the high altar).

Iglesia de San Felipe★ – A fine example of 14C Mudéjar architecture with its handsome tower, interior *artesonado* work bearing the coat of arms of the Hurtado de Mendoza family, and a chancel adorned with colourful 16C *azulejos*.

Plaza Mayor or Plaza de San Fernando – This attractive square is fronted by elegant Mudéjar and Renaissance mansions.

Ayuntamiento – The interesting Baroque town hall in the heart of the old quarter has preserved a peaceful inner patio and an attractive Roman **mosaic**.

Iglesia del Salvador – The handsome plaza de Cristo Rey is fronted by this large Baroque building with a Latin-cross ground plan constructed between the 17C and 19C on top of the remains of an earlier church. Note the impressive Churrigueresque **altarpiece** and the interesting collection of paintings, retables and religious gold and silverware from the 17C and 18C.

Iglesia de Santa María la Mayor* – This large 15C Gothic church was built on the site of the former mosque in the lively calle San Ildefonso. Despite its restoration in Renaissance and Baroque style, the Patio de los Naranjos (Orange Tree Patio), which was part of the original Moorish building, and some beautiful horseshoe arches have been preserved. The 6C **Visigothic calendar**, on the shaft of one of the columns, is particularly interesting.

The triple-nave interior is dominated by a monumental **Plateresque altarpiece*** depicting exquisitely sculpted scenes of the Passion. The side chapels also contain magnificent retables – such as the Christ of the Martyrs – visible behind 16C **Plateresque grilles** designed according to a precise iconographic plan. The sacristy houses a valuable collection of gold and silverwork, including a Renaissance-style processional monstrance, a work by Alfaro.

Convento de las Descalzas* – This magnificent example of 18C Sevillian Baroque has a Latin-cross ground plan, a tower with a double campanile and *azulejo* decoration.

Convento de Santa Clara – The Convent of St Clare was founded in the middle of the 15C. It is embellished by two pleasant cloisters and an attractive Mudéjar church with several canvases by Valdés Leal, as well as a fine collection of female portraits in the style of Zurbarán.

Alcázar de Arriba – This old Roman fortress offers superb **views*** of the countryside around Carmona. It was extended by the Almoravids, and later converted into the palace of Pedro I. Only a few sections of wall, the odd tower and the parade ground, where a **parador** now stands, have been preserved from the original building and enclosure.

Roman necropolis* – *At the end of calle Jorge Bonsor. Access is indicated on the road to Sevilla.* This impressive archaeological site, one of the most important in Andalucía, dates from the 1C AD. Over 300 tombs, mausoleums and cremation kilns have been discovered here, most of which are contained within vaulted funerary chambers with niches for the urns. The most interesting are the **Tumba del Elefante** (so-called on account of the statue of an elephant) with three dining rooms and a kitchen; the

A number of 17C and 18C noble residences are dotted around the town's squares. Of these, the most attractive are the Casa de los **Rueda**, Casa de los **Domínguez**, Casa del **Barón de Gracia Real**, Casa del **Marqués del Saltillo**, Casa de los **Lasso** and the Casa de las **Aguas**. These elegant mansions add a refined air to Carmona and provide an interesting contrast with the older buildings in the heart of the old quarter.

Tumba de Servilia, which is the size of a patrician villa; the columbarium and a large circular mausoleum. Other discoveries found within the confines of the necropolis include an amphitheatre and an interesting collection of items unearthed here, displayed in a small museum.

View of the Old Quarter

Imagen © TURISMO ANDALUZ S.A.

Around Carmona

Viso del Alcor

12km/8mi SW along the A 392.
This town of Celtic origin is located at the highest point in the Sierra de los Alcores. Viso's major architectural feature is the **Iglesia de Santa María del Alcor**, a fine example of late-Mudéjar style, with three aisles with pointed vaulting and a sober Renaissance cupola in the presbytery. It houses a statue of Santa María del Alcor and an interesting collection of 17C paintings from the Venetian School. The 15C **Iglesia de la Merced** is also noteworthy for its unusual collection of 17C and 18C pictorial and sculpted altarpieces.

Mairena del Alcor

16km/10mi SW along the A 392.
Mairena del Alcor is a peaceful small town of whitewashed houses nestled on a small plain and protected by the remains of a Moorish fortress, of which only the the odd tower and an access gateway remain. The town's main attraction is the excessively restored, Mudéjar-style **Iglesia de la Asunción**. The interior of the church contains a handsome 17C-18C **main altarpiece** and several Baroque paintings hanging in the sacristy.

Alcolea del Río

17km/10.5mi N. Take the SE 112 towards Guadajoz then bear onto the SE 129.
Situated on the banks of the Guadalquivir, between the Sierra Morena and the flat landscapes of the Sevillian countryside, Alcolea has two windmills, the Molino de la Aceña and the Molino de la Peña de la Sal, which bear witness to the town's past reliance on the river as a source of income. Alcolea has two churches of note: the Iglesia del Cristo, an 18C Baroque building; and the **Iglesia de San Juan Bautista**, a fine example of 15C Mudéjar architecture housing the image of the Virgen del Consuelo (Virgin of Solace), the town's patron saint.

Écija ★

91km/57mi SW of Sevilla along the A 4 towards Sevilla. Écija stands on the left bank of the River Genil, in the depression of the Bética mountain range. 🅴 *Plaza de España, I,* ☏ *955 90 29 33.*

This elegant town dotted with churches, convents, palaces, and mansions emblazoned with family coats of arms, is recognisable from afar by the silhouette of its numerous bell towers. The "frying pan of Andalucía", a nickname resulting from the extreme heat experienced here in summer, reached its economic peak in the 18C, a period which saw the construction of its major monuments. The beauty of the town's towers and belfries resulted in the influence of the Baroque style so popular in Écija extending to the surrounding area. The writer Luis Vélez de Guevara (1579-1644), the author of *El Diablo Cojuelo*, was born in Écija.
Follow signs to the town centre (centro ciudad) and leave your car in plaza de España.

Plaza de España

This pleasant and spacious landscaped square, popularly known as **El Salón** (Drawing Room) is the hub of Écija life. Three major buildings line the square: the **Iglesia de Santa Bárbara**, with its impressive choir stalls; the **Convento de San Francisco**, with houses backing onto the church; and the town hall *(ayuntamiento)*.

Ayuntamiento – The chapter house contains two **Roman mosaics★**. The 16C coffered wooden ceiling was transferred here from the Convento de San Pablo y Santo Domingo.

Churches and convents; towers and belfries★

The centre of Écija is embellished with a large number of religious buildings.

Torre de San Juan★ – The 18C tower crowning the Church of St John is, without doubt, one of the most beautiful in Écija. Note the delicacy of its Baroque decoration, due to the predominant use of *azulejos*. The result is both elegant and graceful.

Iglesia de Santiago★ – The Church of St James displays a combination of styles: the portal leading to the atrium and the tower are both Baroque, while the remainder of the church is of Gothic-Mudéjar construction with later modifications. The interior comprises three harmoniously proportioned aisles with wooden ceilings, with the exception of the

FESTIVALS

September is the month *par excellence* for fiestas in Écija. The 8th of the month sees a solemn procession in honour of the town's patron saint, the Virgen del Valle (Virgin of the Valley), while around the 21st the Feria de San Mateo is held, with its traditional fiestas, bullfights, demonstrations of horsemanship etc. The Festival de Cante Jondo, meanwhile, attracts leading performers in the world of flamenco to Écija.

Good Friday procession

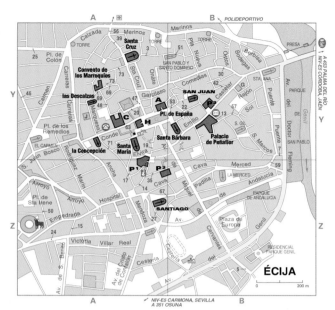

ÉCIJA

apse, which is crowned with Gothic vaulting. The Gothic **retable*** at the high altar illustrates the Passion and the Resurrection of Christ.

Iglesia de Santa María – This church, fronting plaza de Santa María, was erected in the 18C. The handsome Baroque portal is crowned by a large arch and a **tower**, also Baroque, adorned with blue *azulejo* decoration. A series of archaeological items are on display in the cloisters.

Convento de las Teresas – The convent, which occupies a 14C-15C Mudéjar palace, has a fine stone **portal** with *alfiz*, heraldic and rope decoration.

Iglesia de la Concepción – Access to the church is through a simple, red-brick Renaissance doorway. The fine Mudéjar-style *artesonado* work on the interior is worthy of particular note.

Iglesia de los Descalzos – The sober exterior gives no indication of the exuberant decoration which reigns in the **interior*** of this church. The building is a magnificent example of Écija Baroque, with fine **stuccowork** covering the vaults, the cupola above the transept and sections of wall.

Convento de los Marroquíes – The convent is famous for its **belfry***, which locals consider to be the most beautiful in the town, and for the *marroquíes* biscuits still produced and sold by the nuns here.

Iglesia de Santa Cruz – This unusual edifice stands on the plaza de la Virgen del Valle. Upon entering the church, note the series of patio-like areas formed by the walls and arches of an earlier church. The harmonious Renaissance tower with its attractive ceramic decoration is also impressive. The church itself is neo-Classical in style with a Greek-cross ground plan. The interior contains the 13C image of the **Virgin of the Valley**, the patron saint of Écija, as well as a 5C **palaeo-Christian sarcophagus***, depicting themes from the Old Testament, at one of the altars.

Palaces*

A wander through the streets of the town will reveal interesting examples of popular architecture, with inlaid columns on the corners of buildings, houses adorned with coats of arms, patios, and small squares fronted by fine civil edifices.

Palacio de Peñaflor – The palace is now used as a cultural centre. It has a large, original and slightly curved **façade*** with an iron balcony and fresco decoration. The handsome pink marble doorway with its Doric and Solomonic columns and heraldic insignia is particularly impressive.

Palacio de Valdehermoso – *Calle Caballeros*. The bottom section of the fine 16C **Plateresque façade*** is noteworthy for its column shafts, which are of Roman origin.

Palacio de Benamejí – *Calle Cánovas del Castillo*. This elegant 18C brick and marble palace is Baroque in style and comprises two storeys with towers on its corners. The marble **doorway*** consists of a delicate and continuous series of curves which are visible on the mouldings, the balcony and in the general layout of the building. A large escutcheon is the crowning feature of the palace, which now houses the **Museo Histórico Municipal**.

Palacio de los Marqueses de Santaella – *Close to the Palacio de Benamejí. Permission required for access.* It is well worth passing through the simple entrance of the palace to admire the magnificent **fresco-adorned cupola*** above the staircase.

Marchena

66km/41mi E of Sevilla along the A 92 and A 364. Population: 18 018. Marchena is at the heart of an area of great archaeological interest boasting a number of settlements dating back to the Bronze Age. It lies 7.5km/4.5mi N of the A 92 linking Granada and Sevilla.
🛈 *Calle San Francisco, 43,*
☎ *955 84 61 67.*

This small town in the Sevillian countryside enjoyed its period of greatest splendour in the 15C and 16C under the Dukes of Arcos, although its imposing towers, part of the walls that once encircled the town, date from Moorish times. The monument of greatest interest in Marchena is without doubt the magnificent Iglesia de San Juan Bautista.

Arco de la Rosa

This 15C arch was a gateway which punctuated the walls surrounding the town. It consists of a horseshoe arch framed by two rectangular bastions. Note the old section of wall still standing next to it.

Iglesia de San Juan Bautista**

The Church of John the Baptist was built in the 15C in Gothic-Mudéjar style. It fronts a pleasant square with several seigniorial doorways. The sober façade is crowned by a bell tower topped by a spire bearing *azulejo* decoration.

The **interior** comprises five aisles: the three central ones have *artesonado* ceilings, while the two side aisles — extensions which were added during the 16C — are covered by arris vaults. The most surprising feature of the interior is the quality and quantity of **works of art** adorning the walls.

In the presbytery, an outstanding, sumptuously carved and painted **retable***** narrating scenes from the life of Christ is a work created in the early 16C, with paintings by Alejo Fernández and sculptural groups by his brother, Jorge. The 16C **grille** enclosing the high altar was produced by a local workshop. The wrought-iron pulpits are 18C, as is the impressive **grille** in front of the choir. The magnificent mahogany and cedar **choir stalls*** were carved in the 18C by Jerónimo de Balbás; male saints are represented in the upper choir, while the busts of female saints can be seen in small medallions in the upper part of the lower choir. The church's two organs, one Rococo, the other neo-Classical, stand on either side of the choir.

The Capilla del Sagrario, a chapel to the left of the presbytery, is presided over by a magnificent 16C **carved retable**** by Roque Balduque and Jerónimo Hernández. Note the unusual arrangement of the Last Supper at its centre.

The church also contains several noteworthy statues, including an *Immaculate Conception* by Pedro de Mena *(the first chapel in the Epistle nave)* and a *St Joseph and Child (the chapel to the right of the apse)*; it is known that the figure of St Joseph at least is a work by Pedro Roldán.

Museo Zurbarán ★★ − *Entry through the church.* ☎ *955 84 61 67 (Tourist Office).*
The canvases displayed were commissioned for the church sacristy and date from almost the same period as those in the Monasterio de Guadalupe, in the province of Cáceres. Nine paintings by this master-

. Kaufmann/MICHELIN

Iglesia de San Juan Bautista

ful Baroque artist (1598-1664) are exhibited in the museum: *Christ*, *The Immaculate Conception*, *St Peter*, *St James*, *John the Evangelist*, *John the Baptist*, *St Paul*, *St Andrew* and *St Bartholomew*. The church's monstrance and several choir books from the museum's collection are also displayed.

An interesting collection of 16C and 17C embroidery and silverware is exhibited in a separate room.

Head up to the highest part of the town.

Plaza Ducal

This square occupies the site of the former castle parade ground. It is lined by the 18C former town hall with its sober stone doorway.

Nearby, the remains of the castle can be seen, some of which are well preserved and others in ruins. Pass through the Arco de la Alcazaba, an arch dating from the 11C.

Iglesia de Santa María la Mayor or Iglesia de la Mota

The church was built within the confines of the ducal palace. It is a sombre Gothic-Mudéjar construction which was later modified, as can be seen on the tower. The façade consists of a single trumpet-shaped doorway with jagged decoration.

Other interesting buildings in the vicinity include the **Iglesia de San Agustín**, a church built during the transition from Baroque to neo-Classical, and the **Puerta de Morón**, a large fortified tower that now houses the tourist office and a museum dedicated to a local sculptor..

Imagen © TURISMO ANDALUZ S.A.

Door in the old fortified wall

*A*round Marchena

Paradas
8km/5mi SW along the SE 217. Paradas owes its name to its function as a stopping-point *(parada)* for caravans travelling to Sevilla during the Middle Ages. The main attraction of this small town is the **Iglesia de San Eutropio**, whose **museum** contains an interesting collection of religious gold and silverware, illuminated books, and an outstanding *Magdalena* by El Greco.

El Arahal
15km/9.5mi SW along the SE 217. This tranquil town of Moorish origin has conserved an attractive old quarter where small whitewashed houses stand alongside elegant Baroque and neo-Classical buildings. The Capilla de la Vera Cruz, an 18C chapel built in colonial style, is particularly worthy of note, as are three churches: the Mudéjar Iglesia de Nuestra Señora de la Victoria; the 17C **Iglesia de Santa María Magdalena**, with its fine set of choral books and various pieces of silverware; and the **Iglesia de San Roque**, containing several 18C altar-pieces in its side chapels and at the main altar.

Morón de la Frontera
27km/17mi S. Follow the A 364 to Montepalacio, then bear onto the A 361. Morón de la Frontera is an agricultural town extending around the ruins of a Moorish castle, with a military base nearby. Of interest are the **Iglesia de San Miguel**, a Gothic church with a neo-Classical portal and an interior with decorative 18C Baroque features; the **Iglesia de San Ignacio**, also known as the Iglesia de la Compañía as it was built by the Jesuit order, housing an outstanding set of Flemish canvases; and the 16C **Iglesia de San Francisco**, a Renaissance church containing several paintings by the artist **José Ribera**, "Lo Spagnoletto".

Osuna★★

EXCURSIONS

92km/58mi from Sevilla along the A 92. Population: 17 306. Osuna rises above a gently undulating landscape to the south of the Guadalquivir depression, near the A 92 highway linking Sevilla with Granada.
🛈 *Plaza Mayor,* ☎ *954 81 57 32.*

This elegant Andalusian town, built on a hill at the heart of the Sevillian countryside, has preserved a beautiful **monumental centre*** inherited from its former status as a ducal seat. The dukedom was created in 1562 and the House of Osuna was to become one of the most powerful on the Iberian Peninsula. The prosperity that Osuna enjoyed in subsequent centuries is reflected in the fine examples of civil and religious architecture embellishing the town.

Monumental centre*
Follow signs to the town centre (centro ciudad) and Zona Monumental.
Colegiata* – ☎ *954 81 04 44. Open for religious services.* This imposing 16C Renaissance-style collegiate church stands impressively above the town. The façade is adorned with a handsome, finely sculpted Plateresque doorway.

The **church** is composed of three elegant Renaissance aisles opening out onto several chapels and a Baroque apse with an interesting retable in the same style, bearing the coat of arms of the House of Osuna. The organ dates from the 18C.

Several important works of art are on display within its walls: *Jesus of Nazareth* by the "divine" Morales; a *Christ of Mercy* by Juan de Mesa; the superb tenebrist canvas, **The Expiration of Christ****, by **José Ribera**, "lo Spagnoletto"; and an unusually small 16C organ, which is carried during religious processions.

The **sacristy** is adorned with 16C *azulejos* and some original *artesonado* work. Exhibits include several books of Gregorian chants dating from the 16C, and four more **paintings by Ribera****: *St Jerome, The Tears of St Peter, The Martyrdom of St Bartholomew* and *The Martyrdom of St Sebastian*, all of which were painted between 1616 and 1618.

AN EVENTFUL HISTORY

Initially inhabited by the Iberians, who named it Urso, this elegant town was subsequently conquered by the Romans, under Caesar. Following the period of Moorish occupation, it was reconquered by Fernando III the Saint in 1239, and then ceded to the Order of Calatrava by Alfonso X the Wise in 1264. However, its period of greatest splendour is inextricably linked with the House of Osuna, under whose control it passed in 1562, when Felipe II granted the title of Duke of Osuna to the fifth Count of Ureña. The dukedom was responsible for the embellishment of Osuna, as well as its artistic and cultural development.

Additional works of art on view in other rooms include an *Immaculate Conception* by Alonso Cano, a silver processional cross (1534), Flemish paintings, gold and silver and vestments dating from the period in which the Colegiata was founded.

The **Ducal Pantheon★★** was built in Plateresque style in 1545 as the burial place for the Dukes of Osuna. It is approached by a delightful patio, designed in the same style. The chapel stands just below the Colegiata's main altar, and despite its tiny dimensions (8m/26ft long, 4.5m/15ft wide and 2.5m/8ft high), it comprises three aisles and a choir. It is crowned by a blue and gold polychrome coffered ceiling which has been blackened by candle smoke. The altarpiece, by Roque Balduque, represents the Burial of Christ.

The **crypt** beneath the chapel contains the tombs of the most notable Dukes of Osuna and the founders of the Colegiata (the parents of the first duke).

Antigua Universidad – The old university, created in 1548 and in existence until 1824, was founded by Juan Téllez, the Count of Ureña and father of the first Duke of Osuna. It is a large square building made of stone; the circular towers on its corners are crowned by spires decorated with blue and white *azulejos*. Note also the attractive inner patio.

Monasterio de la Encarnación★ – ☎ *954 81 11 21*. This convent of discalced nuns was founded by the fourth Duke of Osuna in the 17C. Its outstanding feature is the magnificent **dado★** of 17C Sevillian *azulejos* in the patio, dedicated to the five senses. This decoration continues up the stairs and on the patio's upper floor. The large collection of paintings, statuary and other objects of artistic interest includes a set of statues of the Infant Jesus, various pieces of gold and silverwork and an 18C Baroque altarpiece. The church is also Baroque in style.

Like many convents in Andalucía, the nuns here produce and sell several types of delicious biscuits and pastries.

Torre del Agua – *On the way down to the plaza Mayor.* ☎ *954 81 12 07*. This medieval defensive tower dates from the 12C-13C, although its origins can be traced to the Carthaginians. Nowadays, it is home to the town's **archaeological museum**, displaying a range of Iberian and Roman objects discovered in Osuna, as well as reproductions of Iberian bulls and Roman bronzes (the originals can be seen in the Museo Arqueológico Nacional, Madrid).

The town

The centre of Osuna has some fine examples of civil architecture, including an impressive array of Baroque **palaces and seigniorial residences★★**.

Calle San Pedro★ – In addition to several interesting town houses and churches, this street contains two magnificent palaces:

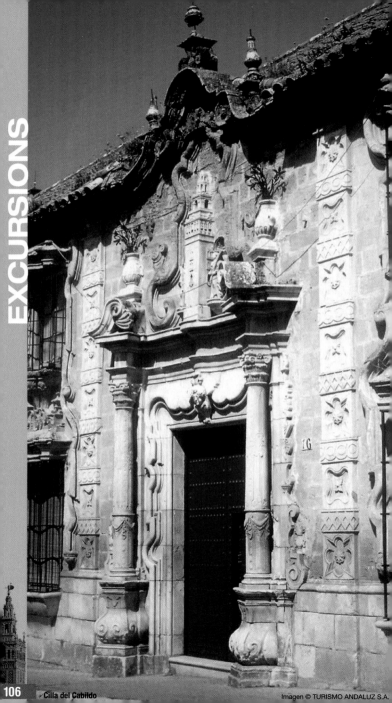

Cilla del Cabildo

The **Cilla del Cabildo** is an original 18C Baroque edifice designed by Alonso Ruiz Florindo, the architect responsible for the tower (torre) of the Iglesia de la Merced (see below). In both buildings he incorporated unusual pilasters with individual decoration. Above the doorway, a somewhat curious copy of the Giralda (Sevilla) dominates the façade.

The **Palacio de los Marqueses de la Gomera**, an 18C Baroque palace, has a striking cornice with a sense of movement created by volutes and waves, in addition to a beautiful stone doorway crowned by a large escutcheon. The building now houses a hotel and restaurant (see Directory).

Antiguo Palacio de Puente Hermoso – Sevilla, 44. The handsome 18C Baroque **portal**★ adorning the façade of this former palace is embellished by the Solomonic columns on the lower tier adorned with fig leaves and bunches of grapes.

The street has several other notable civil and religious buildings.

Palacio de los Cepeda – Calle de la Huerta. This palace is now the home of the town's law courts. It is a handsome 18C construction with an impressive main doorway and a fine cornice crowning the building. However, its most outstanding features are the estípites on the doorway and, in particular, the large coat of arms with the two halberdiers flanking it.

Antigua Audiencia – Carrera Caballos, 82. Osuna's law courts were formerly housed in this sober building dating from the reign of Carlos III.

Torre de la Iglesia de la Merced★ – The church tower, designed by the same architect as the Cilla del Cabildo, is an impressive monument with a number of decorative elements.

Osuna's religious architecture is represented by numerous convents and churches (Santo Domingo, la Compañía, la Concepción etc), predominantly dating from the 17C and 18C.

Parque Natural de la Sierra Norte de Sevilla

This area of outstanding natural beauty is situated in an attractive section of the Sierra Morena mountain range to the north of Sevilla, and borders the provinces of Huelva and Córdoba, as well as the region of Extremadura. The itinerary suggested below starts in the town of Lora del Río, 63km/39mi NE of Sevilla. Follow the A 4 to Carmona and then the A 457.

🛈 *The* **Centro de Información** *in Constantina is able to provide maps and information on all the activities available within the park.* ☎ *955 88 15 97.*

The park covers an area of 164 840ha/407 320 acres in the section of the Sierra Morena to the north of Sevilla. It is dissected by several rivers, including the Viar, Huéznar and Retortillo, which have created a lush vegetation abounding in cork oak, horse chestnut, elm, holm oak and hazel along their courses. The park's fauna is equally rich, with the presence of wild boar, harrier eagles and tawny vultures, to name but a few species.

From Lora del Río to Guadalcanal: 90km/56mi – allow one day.

Lora del Río

Situated outside the boundaries of the park. This irregularly shaped town is situated on the right bank of the Guadalquivir, at the base of the foothills of the Sierra Morena. Lora is a peaceful place steeped in tradition, whose carefully maintained streets and buildings lend it a slightly serious air.

Local delicacies include snails *(caracoles)*, *sopeaos* (a variant of the traditional *gazpacho*), and the popular *gachas con coscurros*, a flour-based purée sprinkled with breadcrumbs fried in olive oil.

Iglesia de la Asunción – This Mudéjar-Gothic church was built in the 15C on the remains of the former mosque, although it has since undergone considerable restoration. Its bell tower, added in the 19C, is one of the tallest in Sevilla province.

Ayuntamiento – The 18C Baroque town hall has a magnificent **façade** with floral decoration.

Casa de los Leones – This fine example of Baroque civil architecture has an impressive façade and an elegant internal patio.

Casa de la Virgen – The doorway of this unusual late-18C palace is embellished with elegant marble columns.

Santuario de Nuestra Señora de Setefilla – This handsome Mudéjar sanctuary, rebuilt in the 17C, stands in an isolated mountain landscape on the outskirts of Lora del Río. Inside is the statue of the highly venerated Virgin of Setefilla, in whose honour a lively pilgrimage *(romería)* is held on 8 September every year.

Constantina

29km/18mi N along the A 455. The town, situated in a beautiful **setting** surrounded by delightful forests and streams of crystal-clear water, owes its name to the Roman emperor Constantine. Its centre is a mix of Moorish buildings and 15C-17C noble edifices which add a touch of distinction to the town.

Barrio de la Morería* – The town's Moorish quarter sits at the foot of the old fortress perched above Constantina. Its steep, narrow and winding alleyways lined by whitewashed houses and connected by numerous flights of steps have preserved all the enchantment and flavour of a typical Arab district. Amid this labyrinth, two churches are worthy of note: the impressive **Iglesia de la Encarnación**, an elegant Mudéjar construction with a handsome Plateresque façade on which the portal (Puerta del Pardón) is adorned with outstanding stone decorative motifs, including a delicate sculpture of the archangel Gabriel; and the **Iglesia de Nuestra Señora de los Dolores**, which has preserved its notable Renaissance cloisters and an interesting Baroque retable at the high altar.

Ermita de El Robledo – *5km/3mi NE along the SE 150.* Within this white Mudéjar chapel, set amid an isolated landscape, is the statue of the Virgin of the Oak Wood *(robledo).*

El Pedroso

18km/11mi W of Constantina along the A 452. The town of El Pedroso, set in a landscape of outstanding beauty, has two impressive religious buildings: the Ermita de San Sebastián and the Iglesia de Nuestra Señora del Pino. The **views** of the surrounding mountains from the nearby hills of Monteagudo and La Lima are quite delightful.

Cazalla de la Sierra

17km/10.5mi N along the A 432. This delightful small town is hidden away in the heart of the Sierra Morena amid a landscape of holm and cork oak forests. The centre of Cazalla is characterised by picturesque streets fronted by attractive seigniorial houses with elegant stone façades. The town is renowned for its brandies.

Plaza Mayor – This extensive rectangular square, the hub of local life, is bordered

CEP MUSHROOMS

The area around Constantina is a paradise for mushroom-lovers. During the autumn, the town is inundated by visitors who come here to pick them or simply to enjoy them in one of Constantina's many bars and restaurants.

by an impressive array of 16C popular Andalusian architecture. Also lining the square are the law courts *(Juzgado)* – note the handsome Baroque façade – and the 14C **Iglesia de Nuestra Señora de la Consolación**, crowned by a red-brick Mudéjar tower adorned with pointed and trefoil arch windows. The church interior is a mass of pillars, topped by Renaissance coffered vaults.

Convento de San Francisco – The outstanding Baroque cloisters are embellished with graceful columns supporting semicircular arches.

Ruinas de la Cartuja – *3km/1.8mi N.* The monumental ruins of the former 15C Carthusian monastery are situated in an attractive setting of leafy woodland. The Mudéjar paintings in the cloisters are of particular note. The former monk-gatekeeper's lodge has been transformed into a small hotel.

Imagen © TURISMO ANDALUZ S.A.

Alanís

17km/10.5mi N of Cazalla along the A 432. Alanís stands at the heart of an impregnable mountain area, at the foot of the remains of its medieval castle. The main buildings of interest here are the Casa de Doña Matilde Guitart, with its elegant two-storey patio, and in particular the **Iglesia de Nuestra Señora de las Nieves**, a Gothic church that has been rebuilt in neo-Classical style. The vault above the high altar is decorated with an attractive set of frescoes, and some exceptional Mudéjar **azulejos** are on view in the 16C Capilla de los Melgarejo.

Guadalcanal

11km/7mi NW along the A 432. This old fortified settlement has preserved interesting vestiges of its medieval walls. The Iglesia de la Asunción, a church built above the former Moorish mosque, and the Ermita de Guaditoca, a chapel which hosts an important pilgrimage, are its most outstanding architectural features.

Utrera ★

37km/23mi SW of Sevilla along the A 376. Population: 45. Utrera stands at the crossroads of the A 376, running SE from Sevilla to Ronda, and the A 364, heading SW to Jerez de la Frontera.

Rodrigo Caro, 3, ☎ 955 86 09 31.

Utrera is built on a small elevation at the heart of the Sevillian countryside, amid a landscape of eucalyptus groves and extensive areas of cultivated land. Although its origins date back to Roman times, its main period of development took place from the 16C onwards. A serious epidemic stunted this expansion in the middle of the 17C, heralding a decline that continued until the 19C. Despite these setbacks, the historical centre of this elegant town has preserved a number of noteworthy monuments.

Castle

This fortress of Almohad origin formed part of the walled defensive system surrounding the town. Today, only a few sections of the walls and an arch, the Arco de la Villa, to which an upper, chapel-like section was added in the 18C, remain from the original structure. An impressive keep and parade ground can also be seen within the castle's confines.

Iglesia de Santa María de la Asunción or Iglesia de Santa María de la Mesa ★

This Gothic church with additional Renaissance and Baroque features dominates a charming square in the centre of the town. The handsome façade is articulated around a large splayed arch, above which rises a graceful Baroque tower. The outstanding features inside include the **choir stalls**, a work by Duque Cornejo (1744), the main altarpiece and the noteworthy sepulchre of the Count of Arcos.

Iglesia de Santiago

This triple-nave Gothic church dates from the 15C. Its severe, defensive look contrasts with the ostentatious decor of the **Puerta del Perdón**, an Isabelline-Gothic-style gateway with an abundance of floral ornamentation.

Plaza del Altozano ★

This elegant square stands at the heart of Utrera. It is framed by an attractive series of three-storey 17C and 18C mansions with two-sided roofs and delicate unbroken balconies.

Ayuntamiento

The town hall is situated on one side of the elegant plaza de Gibaxa. This old 18C palatial mansion has a magnificent Rococo façade and a number of rooms with a romantic air.

Note also the collection of furniture in the Salón Azul (Blue Room).

Casa Surga

This late-18C mansion has a charming Baroque façade and rooms decorated according to the tastes of the period.

Iglesia de San Francisco

The main feature of this 17C late-Renaissance church is the large cupola adorned with paintings.

Santuario de Nuestra Señora de la Consolación*

This outstanding 17C and 18C Mudéjar-style sanctuary occupies a former Franciscan monastery. The impressive Baroque façade and the delicate *artesonado* work inside the sanctuary are particularly worthy of note. On 8 September a popular pilgrimage *(romería)* is held here in honour of the Virgin of Solace *(Consolación)*.

El Palmar de Troya

13km/8mi S along the A 364.
The heretical Order of the Carmelites of the Holy Face, founded by the controversial priest Clemente Rodríguez, has its headquarters here. The centre of El Palmar is occupied by an enormous church in which statues of various saints, presided over by a sculpture of Our Crowned Lady of El Palmar, are venerated. The best time to visit the church is in the afternoon, when mass is held in Latin in accordance with the liturgy decreed prior to that established by the Second Vatican Council.

Suitable dress: women who wish to attend religious ceremonies at El Palmar de Troya will need to observe a strict dress code which requires them to wear trousers and to cover their head with a veil.

Directory

Transport

Airport – San Pablo international airport (☎ *954 44 90 00*) is located 12km/8mi to the east of the city along the N IV towards Madrid. In addition to taxis, a bus service operates to the city centre and Santa Justa railway station *(cost: €2.30)*.

Trains – The Santa Justa railway station is on avenida Kansas City. There are regular departures throughout the province, as well as to the rest of Spain, including the famous AVE high-speed train, which connects Sevilla with Madrid in just 2hr 25min and Córdoba in 45min. Information and reservations, ☎ 902 24 02 02.

Inter-city buses – Sevilla has two bus stations:
- Estación de Plaza de Armas *(plaza de Armas)*: services to the rest of the province, Huelva, elsewhere in Spain, Portugal and other European countries, ☎ 954 90 77 37/80 40.
- Estación de El Prado de San Sebastián *(prado de San Sebastián)*: departures across Andalucía, ☎ 954 41 71 18.

City buses – Operated by **Tussam** (☎ *900 71 01 71*). These offer the best way of getting around the city. A single journey costs €1, although it is possible to purchase a 10-trip *abono de diez viajes* costing €4.60 (including the option to transfer from one line to another within one hour) or €3.90 (excluding the transfer option).

Taxis – ☎ 954 58 00 00 and 954 62 22 22.

Sightseeing

Publications – Two free bilingual publications (Spanish-English) are published for tourists every month. These brochures, **Welcome Olé** and **The Tourist**, can be obtained from major hotels and tourist sites around the city.

Sevilla City Hall's Department of Culture **(NODO)** also publishes a monthly brochure listing all the city's cultural events. A monthly publication covering the whole of Andalucía, **El Giraldillo**, contains information on the region's fairs, exhibitions and theatres, as well as details on cinemas, restaurants and shops. *www.elgiraldillo.es*

Horse-drawn carriages – This alternative form of transport is a pleasant way of discovering the major sites of the city. Carriages can normally be hired in plaza de la Virgen de los Reyes, plaza de España, avenida de la Constitución and at the Torre del Oro.

Boat trips on the Guadalquivir – Departures every half-hour from the Torre del Oro, offering visitors to Sevilla a different view of the city. It is also possible to take a trip to the mouth of the river at Sanlúcar de Barrameda, passing the Parque Nacional de Doñana en route.

Tourist bus – The *bus turístico* offers regular circuits of the city's main sights, stopping at each of them, enabling passengers to get on and off at leisure. Departures from the Torre del Oro.

Where to Eat

The restaurants listed in this section have been chosen for their surroundings, ambience, typical dishes or unusual character. Prices specified correspond to the average cost of both an inexpensive and expensive meal and are given as a guideline only. Restaurants are classified into three categories based on price:

- Budget: under €15 (See Tapas)
- Moderate: between €15 and €30
- Expensive: over €30

Bodegón La Universal – *Betis, 2 (Triana)* – ☎ *954 33 47 46* – 🖩 – *€17/31* – *Closed Wed*. The terrace, cooled by the fresh air rising from the Guadalquivir, provides a great view of the city and bullring. Traditional cuisine and a pleasant place to eat either before or after exploring the Triana quarter.

La Albahaca – *Plaza de Santa Cruz, 12* – ☎ *954 22 07 14* – 🖩 – *€33/42* – *Closed Sun*. If you decide to eat in this former seigniorial mansion, you can select your table from a choice of three dining rooms. International cuisine. Outdoor terrace for the summer months.

El Burladero – *Canalejas, 1* – ☎ *954 50 55 99* – 🖩 – *€36/49* – *Closed 15 Jul-Aug*. A popular, top-class restaurant and tapas bar. Sober, yet refined decor. The house speciality here is *rabo de toro* (braised bull's tail).

Taberna del Alabardero – *Zaragoza, 20* – ☎ *954 50 27 21* – 🖩 – *€47* – *Closed Aug*. This 19C mansion houses one of the best restaurants in Sevilla, a seven-room hotel, a pleasant tea room and the city's school of hotel management. Well worth a visit just to admire the decor.

magen © TURISMO ANDALUZ S.A.

Tapas

It is rare for tapas bars to list prices. Tapas or the larger *raciones* can vary enormously from one bar to the next, although as a general rule the standard is generally good, with prices rarely exceeding €15 per person for an informal meal.

Calle Mateos Gago – *(Santa Cruz)*. This tourist street close to the Giralda is full of bars and restaurants. One of these is the **Bodega de Santa Cruz**, popular with Sevilla's young crowd who spill out onto the street, eating and drinking. The **La Giralda** *cervecería (at n°1)* is one of this district's most traditional bars, offering a good choice of tasty *raciones*. A little further up the street is the **Bodega Belmonte** *(at n°24)*, a new bar already known for its delicious *lomo a la pimienta* (spicy loin of pork).

Las Teresas – *Santa Teresa, 2 (Santa Cruz)*. This small, typically Sevillian tavern, whose doors open onto a picturesque narrow street, is one of the oldest in the Barrio Santa Cruz. Attractive early-19C decor and delicious tapas. The **Casa Plácido** opposite is a good place for cold tapas.

Puerta de la Carne – *Santa María La Blanca, 36 (Santa Cruz)*. A perfect location to discover one of Sevilla's most original traditions: the eating of all kinds of seafood and fried fish served, ready to eat, in paper cones.

Kiosco de Las Flores – *Plaza del Altozano (Triana)*. A tapas bar next to the Puente de Triana, with a terrace close to the Guadalquivir. Run by the same family since 1930, it specialises in fried fish, seafood and *ortiguillas* (fried seaweed).

Sol y Sombra – *Castilla, 149–151 (Triana) – Closed Mon, Tue lunchtime and in Aug.* One of the most popular bars in the city. This bustling bar with its characteristic aromas of fine cheeses, cured hams and cigarette smoke, and walls covered with old and modern brightly coloured bull-fighting posters is a must for visitors.

Casa Cuesta – *Castilla, 3 (Triana) – Closed Tue.* Founded in 1917, this bar specialises in beef dishes. With the onset of fine weather, tables are set out on the small square nearby.

Bodeguita Romero – *Harinas, 10 (Arenal) – Closed Mon (except public hols and in Aug)* Located next to the Maestranza bullring. Famous for its exquisite *pringá* (a meat stew eaten with bread). Popular with the business community at lunchtime.

Casablanca – *Zaragoza, 50 (Plaza Nueva) – Closed Sun.* This small bar, one of the most famous in Sevilla, is always full and is particularly popular with locals.

El Patio de San Eloy – *San Eloy, 9 (Centro)* – ☎ 954 22 11 48. An unusual bar with several distinct sections. As you enter, there is a small wine counter on the right; the central bar offers a wide range of sandwiches (*bocadillos*) from Andalucía, Catalunya, Galicia, France, Belgium etc; while the *azulejo*-adorned benches at the back (similar to those found in an Arab bath) are the ideal place for a chat with friends. Always packed at lunchtime.

El Rinconcillo – *Gerona, 40 (Santa Catalina) – Closed 17 Jul-2 Aug.* One of the oldest and most attractive bars in Sevilla. Although its origins date back to 1670, the current decor is from the 19C, including the attractive *azulejo* panelling and the wooden ceiling and counter.

Bodega Extremeña –*Calle Águilas, on the corner of calle Candilejo (Alfalfa).* An unusual showcase for products from Extremadura in the heart of Andalucia. This small bar serves some excellent cheeses (such as the famous Torta del Casar), hams, and a whole range of sausages, chorizos and wines.

In Carmona

La Almazara de Carmona – *Santa Ana, 33 – ☎ 954 19 00 76 – €25/29.* This bar is housed in an old oil mill. Stylish decor, with its vaults and a wooden ceiling. Local spinach, partridge and suckling pig *(cochinillo)* all feature prominently on the menu.

El Rinconcillo

Imagen © TURISMO ANDALUZ S.A.

Where to Stay

Hotels listed below are divided into three categories based on the price of a single room, excluding VAT (7%), and have been chosen for their location, comfort, good value-for-money, and in some cases, their particular charm. The two prices listed under each hotel represent the cost of a single room in low season and a double room in high season.

- ⊜ Budget: under €50
- ⊜⊜ Moderate: between €50 and €80
- ⊜⊜⊜ Expensive: over €80

Sevilla has a huge range of accommodation for visitors, but beware **Holy Week** and the **Feria**, when prices are likely to double or even triple. If you're planning to stay in the city for these events, make sure you check the room rate carefully beforehand.

⊜ **Londres** – *San Pedro Mártir, 1* – ☎ *954 50 27 45* – *Fax 950 38 30* – *www.londreshotel.com* – ▤ *–25 rooms* – €41/48. Near the Museo de Bellas Artes. This centrally located hotel has basic but clean rooms, some with balcony. The rooms overlooking the street are generally quieter and more pleasant than those to the rear. No lift.

⊜ **Hotel Doña Blanca** – *Plaza Jerónimo de Córdoba, 14* – ☎ *954 50 13 73* – ▤ *– 19 rooms* – €45/67. The rooms at this attractive mansion, with its distinctive red façade, are very reasonably priced given its size, decor and comfort. The other major plus is its central location in a bustling part of the city near the Convento de Santa Paula.

⊜⊜ **Hostal Van Gogh** – *Miguel de Mañara, 4* – ☎ *954 56 37 27* – ▤ *– 14 rooms* – €51/57 *(including VAT)*. Despite its name, this *hostal* is typically Sevillian, with a bull's head over the entrance, brightly coloured walls and pots of geraniums on the balconies. Simple, clean rooms and a good location in the Santa Cruz district.

⊜⊜ **Hotel Simón** – *García Vinuesa, 19* – ☎ *954 22 66 60* – *Fax 954 56 22 41* – ▤ *– 29 rooms* – €50/100 – ☕ €4.20. This whitewashed mansion, arranged around a cool internal patio, seems to be from a different era, with corridors decorated with antique furniture and large mirrors. All the bedrooms are comfortable; the best are decorated with colourful *azulejos*. An excellent location close to the cathedral.

⊜⊜ **Hotel Amadeus** – *Farnesio, 6* – ☎ *954 50 14 43* – *www.hotelamadeussevilla.com* – ▤ *– 14 rooms* – €63/126 – ☕ €7. A family of musicians converted this magnificent mansion in the heart of the Santa Cruz district into this delightful small hotel, in which the luxurious decor enhances the building's original architectural features.

⊜⊜⊜ **Corregidor** – *Morgado, 17* – ☎ *954 38 51 11* – *Fax 954 38 42 38* – ▣ ▤ *–76 rooms, 1 suite* – €100/140 – ☕ €9. This hotel, slightly set back from other buildings in the street, has an attractive façade, large entrance hall, comfortable rooms and a small garden.

⊜⊜⊜ **Casas de la Judería** – *Callejón Dos Hermanas, 7* – ☎ *954 41 51 50* – *Fax 954 42 21 70* – *www.casasypalacios.com* – ▣ ▤ *– 119 rooms* – *from* €87 – ☕ €15. A pleasant surprise in the city's old Jewish quarter. Elegant, traditional and full of colour, this charming, old hotel is housed in the former mansion of the Duke of Béjar.

⊜⊜⊜ **Doña María** – *Don Remondo, 19* – ☎ *954 22 49 90* – *Fax 954 21 95 46* – ▤ *– 64 rooms, 2 suites* – €100/190 – ☕ €12. An old, tastefully renovated building with a view of the Giralda. Even if you're not staying here, it is well worth spending some time on its delightful terrace.

⊖⊕⊕ **Casa Imperial** – *Imperial, 29* – ☎ *954 50 03 00* – *Fax 954 50 03 30* – 🖃 – *18 rooms, 8 suites* – *€230/250 (including breakfast).* The Casa Imperial occupies an interesting Baroque-style mansion in a quiet street behind the Casa de Pilatos. Although its original construction was started in the 16C, the current building dates from the 17C and 18C. Attractive main patio.

⊖⊕⊕ **Alfonso XIII** – *San Fernando, 2* – ☎ *954 91 70 00* – *Fax 954 91 70 99* – 🖃 – *127 rooms* – *19 suites* – *€347/455* – ☕ *€20.* Built in 1928 in neo-Mudéjar style, the Alfonso XIII is Sevilla's most luxurious and famous hotel.

In Carmona

⊖ **Hostal Comercio** – *Torre del Oro, 56* – *b/Fax 954 14 00 18* – 🖃 – *14 rooms* – *€32/45 (including VAT).* The same family has run this small *pensión* dating from the 16C for the past four generations. An attractive patio, and basic but clean rooms.

⊖⊕⊕ **Parador de Carmona** – *In the Alcázar* ☎ *954 14 10 10* – *Fax 954 14 17 12* – 🖃 – *63 rooms* – *€108/135* – ☕ *€11.* This magnificent *parador*, with its superb views of the fertile Corbones plain, is housed in the former residence of the Catholic Monarchs. Even if you don't get the chance to stay here, try and eat in the restaurant, one of the most attractively decorated of the entire Spanish *parador* network. Specialities include Carmona spinach *(espinaca)* and partridge *(perdiz).* Restaurant: approx. €27.

⊖⊕⊕ **Casa de Carmona** – *Plaza de Lasso, 1* – ☎ *954 19 10 00* – *Fax 954 19 01 89* – 🖃 – *32 rooms, 1 suite* – *€215/220 (☕ included).* A charming 16C palace located in the old part of Carmona. Large aristocratic lounges, a patio, fountain and Moorish garden. The building formerly belonged to Lasso de la Vega, the governor of Chile.

In Osuna

⊖ **El Caballo Blanco** – *Granada, 1* – ☎/*Fax 954 81 01 84* – 🖃 – *13 rooms* – *€28/48* – ☕ *€2.90.* This motel-like residence is located in the heart of Osuna. Spotlessly clean rooms, all at street level. Good value for money.

⊖⊕ **Palacio del Marqués de la Gomera** – *San Pedro, 20* – ☎ *954 81 22 23* – *Fax 954 81 02 00* – 🖃 – *18 rooms, 2 suites* – *€75/94* – ☕ *€10.* This 18C architectural jewel, which once belonged to the Marquess of La Gomera, has been transformed into a hotel with rooms that have been tastefully furnished and maintained.

The hotel's **restaurant**, La Casa del Marqués (€27/33), is accessed via an elegant patio. Refined menu of Andalusian cuisine.

In the Sierra Norte

⊖ **Posada del Moro** – *Paseo del Moro, 46* – *Cazalla de la Sierra* – ☎/*Fax 954 88 48 58* – 🖃 – *14 rooms* – *€35/60* – ☕ *€3.* A small, pleasant family-run hotel situated opposite the Parque del Moro. The hotel has a high-quality restaurant and a garden with swimming pool. Good value for money.

⊖ **San Blas** – *Miraflores, 4* – *Constantina* – ☎ *955 88 00 77* – *Fax 955 88 19 00* – 🖃 – *15 rooms* – *€43/59* – ☕ *€6.* A modern building, perhaps lacking in charm, but with spacious, well-appointed rooms. A small swimming pool is open to guests on the terrace.

⊖⊕ **Las Navezuelas** – *Cazalla de la Sierra* – *On the A 432, heading towards El Pedroso; access is via a 500m/550yd dirt track.* – ☎ *954 88 47 64* – *Fax 954 88 45 94* – *www.lasnavezuelas.com* – *6 rooms, 2 suites, 3 apartments* – **P** – *€60/80 (☕ included)* – *Closed 7 Jan-25 Feb.* A small paradise in which, according to its owner "twelve years of effort have been expended" to create the delightful residence visible today. The guest rooms have all been tastefully decorated, while the swimming pool offers a magnificent view of the Sierra Morena. A bucolic setting, where the only sound is the far-off bleating of sheep.

Bars and Cafés

When it comes to nightlife, the most popular areas for a drink are the city centre, particularly around the cathedral, and the attractive Santa Cruz and Arenal districts, all of which provide a magnificent historical backdrop. The working-class district of Triana, in particular calle Betis on the opposite bank of the Guadalquivir, is also lively, with a number of bars and clubs with a local flavour. Sevilla's younger crowd tends to prefer the action in the Nervión district, with its numerous nightclubs, many of which stay open until dawn. The city's alternative crowd heads for Alameda de Hércules, where visitors will need to exercise caution at night, but which is nonetheless home to several interesting haunts, such as Fun Club, a popular concert venue, and the Habanilla café, with its large and unusual collection of old coffee pots.

In summer, the action moves down to the river, where several kilometres of bars and outdoor terraces are popular with people of all ages and tastes.

Horno San Buenaventura – *Avenida de la Constitución, 16 – Open 8am-10pm.* Part of a network of old furnaces *(hornos)* over six centuries old. Particularly popular because of its proximity to the cathedral and its spacious tea-room on the ground floor. Its cakes are justifiably famous.

La Campana – *Plaza de la Campana, 1 – Open 8am-10pm.* One of Sevilla's classic cafeterias. The Rococo decor creates a pleasant atmosphere in which to enjoy La Campana's pastries, which are famous throughout the city. Varied clientele ranging from the district's senior citizens to tourists passing through the centre.

Café de la Prensa – *Betis, 8 – Open 10am-1am.* This modern café with a young and intellectual ambience is located alongside the riverbank. Its outdoor tables offer a magnificent view of both the Guadalquivir and the monumental heart of the city. Perfect for whiling away the late afternoon or for a few drinks to start the evening.

La Campana

Imagen © TURISMO ANDALUZ S.A.

Antigüedades – *Argote de Molina, 40 – Open 8pm-3am*. One of Sevilla's most colourful clubs with decor which changes every month according to what's on. Another haunt popular with the young crowd, particularly thirtysomethings. Very lively around midnight.

Abades – *Abades, 13 – Open 5pm-late*. This 18C palatial residence in the heart of the Barrio Santa Cruz has a number of Baroque lounges filled with antiques. A select clientèle, who can enjoy a relaxing drink in elegant surroundings to the background strains of classical music.

La Carbonería – *Levíes, 18 – Open 8pm-4am*. One of Sevilla's institutions and the key to the culture of the city's alternative crowd. Housed in a former coal warehouse in the Jewish Quarter *(Judería)*, La Carbonería is split up into a number of different areas, where you can listen to a musical recital in intimate surroundings around a chimney or to authentic lively flamenco (live music every night). The venue also hosts art and photography exhibitions. A must!

El Tamboril – *Plaza Santa Cruz – Open 10pm-5am*. Tucked away in a corner of the Santa Cruz district, this *taberna* is always heaving with its faithful clientele who occasionally burst into song with an impromptu *sevillana* or *rumba*. Always busy until the early hours of the morning. The Salve Rociera, a prayer to Our Lady of El Rocío, is sung every day at midnight.

Sala Mandra – *Torneo, 43 – Open Tue-Sat, 10pm-6am*. This modern, industrial-style venue hosts rock and pop concerts every Friday and occasionally on Thursdays, as well as some theatrical events. At the end of shows, the venue reverts to its function as a disco, with Latin sounds on Thursdays and Saturdays and more commercial music on Fridays. The most avant-garde of the city's clubs.

Voulé-Bar / Wall Street – *Calle Balbino Marrón, edificio Viapol – Open Wed-Sat, midnight-6am*. These two adjoining bars are also located in the city's favourite clubbing district for young people, Nervión. **Voulé-Bar** organises regular salsa and flamenco concerts and occasionally books a leading band. At **Wall Street** people order drinks based on the fluctuating prices indicated on the numerous screens all along the bar. Both venues attract huge numbers of people who tend to move back and forth between the two venues throughout the night. Average age between 25 and 35.

Sopa de Ganso – *Calle Pérez Galdós, 8 – Open 1pm-2am, Fri-Sat until 6am*. With its decorative emphasis on wood and its varied play list, the Sopa de Ganso is another popular nightclub. A varied clientele, including a few foreigners, come to enjoy the alternative, yet fun, atmosphere here. Always busy in the afternoon and early evening with people who come here to enjoy the great pastries.

La Sonanta – *Calle San Jacinto, 31 – Open 8.30pm-late*. This small bar across the river in Triana serves tapas by day and fills up with lovers of flamenco by night. Live performances on Thursdays and Fridays. Twice a year La Sonanta organises a flamenco festival. A varied public, ranging from tourists to die-hard flamenco fans.

The **paseo de las Delicias** is home to four venues (Chile, Líbano, Alfonso and Bilindo). Although not open all year round, these venues become lively in summer, when they are perfect for those who prefer to move from bar to bar. On winter afternoons they are ideal for a quiet drink in the middle of the María Luisa park, surrounded by buildings used during the 1929 Ibero-American Exhibition, while in the summer, drinking and dancing outdoors into the early hours is more the scene. The age range is between 25 and 40, but varies from one venue to the next.

Entertainment

Sevilla is a lively and festive capital offering a whole host of varied cultural activities all year round.

The **Teatro de la Maestranza** *(paseo de Colón, 22 – ☏ 954 22 65 73 or 954 22 33 44 – www.maestranza.com)* offers a full season of theatre and dance, including performances by leading international stars, particularly in the field of opera.

The **Teatro Lope de Vega** *(avenida María Luisa – ☏ 954 59 08 53)* tends to concentrate on drama and flamenco.

The modern **Teatro Central** *(avenida José de Gálvez – ☏ 954 46 07 80 – www.teatrocentral.com)*, built for Expo'92 on the Isla de la Cartuja, offers a varied programme of avant-garde theatre, concerts by some of the world's leading opera singers, as well as a season of flamenco.

In addition to the major theatres above, Sevilla has many smaller concert halls and other venues which organise concerts and recitals.

Other cultural aspects are equally well covered in the city, which boasts a number of exhibition halls and galleries devoted to art. The exhibitions organised by the Centro Andaluz de Arte Contemporáneo in the Monasterio de la Cartuja are particularly worthy of note.

Imagen © TURISMO ANDALUZ S.A.

Shopping

Sevilla has a huge range of shops, the most traditional of which are concentrated in the historic centre, particularly along calle Tetuán, in the plaza del Duque de la Victoria, calle de San Eloy and other pedestrian areas in this district. Special mention should be made of the historic **calle Sierpes**, with its variety of traditional and more unusual shops and boutiques, including several Foronda boutiques, selling the hand-embroidered shawls created by this famous local artisan. The Ochoa pastry shop is also located here; this local landmark is a perfect spot for breakfast or for an afternoon snack, but also has an excellent selection of take-away cakes and pastries. The streets at right angles to Sierpes and those around the nearby El Salvador church are very popular, particularly with jewellery hunters, who are spoilt for choice in the plaza del Pan and the calle Alcaicería.

In the **Los Remedios** district on the other side of the river, calle Asunción has a number of leading brand-name stores selling a whole range of goods.

The modern Nervión district is home to two large shopping centres (El Corte Inglés and Nervión Plaza), as well as several stores belonging to leading clothing chains.

Another large shopping centre has been developed in the **former Plaza de Armas railway station**, an interesting regionalist building dating from the beginning of the 20C. Here you will find the La Fábrica de Cerveza, where you can enjoy a beer while at the same time contemplating how it has been made.

Markets – Sevilla has numerous open-air markets, most of which specialise in a particular type of goods. The "jueves" (Thursday) market, in calle Feria, is a popular market for antiques and second-hand goods where you might just pick up an interesting bargain. On Sunday mornings, markets are held in several parts of the city, including plaza de la Alfalfa, a much-frequented livestock market; plaza del Cabildo, with its stalls selling stamps and old coins; and along Alameda de Hércules, where a multitude of temporary stalls selling second-hand goods are set up early in the morning to entice visitors.

In Carmona

No visit to Carmona is complete without buying some of the delicious **pastries** produced by the town's numerous convents. Local specialities here include the sponge-like *bizcochos marroquíes*, the honeyed doughnuts known as *roscos almibarados*, a range of tarts *(tortas)* and *bollos de aceite*, literally "olive oil buns".

Index